O'Shaughnessy - Frey Library
University of St. Thomas
St. Paul, MN 55105

The Sexual Life of Children

The Sexual Life of Children

Floyd M. Martinson

590285

BERGIN & GARVEY
Westport, Connecticut
London

Library of Congress Cataloging-in-Publication Data

Martinson, Floyd Mansfield.
 The sexual life of children / Floyd M. Martinson.
  p. cm.
 Includes bibliographical references and index.
 ISBN 0–89789–376–X (alk. paper)
 1. Children and sex. 2. Children—Sexual behavior. I. Title.
HQ784.S45M37 1994
306.7′083—dc20   93–37847

British Library Cataloguing in Publication Data is available.

Copyright © 1994 by Floyd M. Martinson

All rights reserved. No portion of this book may be
reproduced, by any process or technique, without the
express written consent of the publisher.

Library of Congress Catalog Card Number: 93–37847
ISBN: 0–89789–376–X

First published in 1994

Bergin & Garvey, 88 Post Road West, Westport, CT 06881
An imprint of Greenwood Publishing Group, Inc.

Printed in the United States of America

The paper used in this book complies with the
Permanent Paper Standard issued by the National
Information Standards Organization (Z39.48–1984).

10 9 8 7 6 5 4 3 2 1

Copyright Acknowledgment

The author and publisher gratefully acknowledge permission to reprint material from the
following copyrighted source.

Excerpts from "Current Legal Status of the Erotic and Sexual Rights of Children," by Floyd
M. Martinson, from *Handbook of Sexology: VII Childhood and Adolescent Sexology*, M. E.
Perry, ed., Amsterdam, the Netherlands: Elsevier, 1990.

Contents

Introduction		vii
1.	Early Development and Experience	1
2.	Self-Stimulation	21
3.	Sex Play in Childhood and Preadolescence	35
4.	Same-Sex Sex Play	57
5.	Dreams, Fantasies, and Myths	65
6.	Sexual Encounters with Older Children, Adolescents, and Adults	75
7.	Sexuality Education	101
8.	Children and the Law	119
9.	The Sexual Life of Children: Sweden and the United States	133
Bibliography		139
Index		149

Introduction

There are many aspects to the life of children. The more we take them seriously—the more we relate to them, observe them, study them—the more aspects of their life we come to understand and appreciate. Robert Coles, after a long career of relating to, studying, and writing about children, came to the awareness that there were still perspectives in the life of children that he had not focused on, and he wrote three additional books—*The Political Life of Children* (1986), *The Moral Life of Children* (1986), and *The Spiritual Life of Children* (1990). The book that you now hold in your hands focuses on still another perspective on child life that has received little attention; namely, the sexual life of children.

I first wrote a treatise on the subject twenty years ago. I submitted it to a number of publishers, but none chose to publish it. The scene has changed in the years since; there is interest in the subject today. Currently, there is a surge of interest in attempting to understand all aspects of childhood and the life of children. Childhood has come to be seen not only as a transitional phase in the life of an individual, but children are seen as constituting a distinctive population group in society with their own interests and needs.

It comes as no surprise to mothers of young children that it is now recognized that infants respond to and engage in sensuous experiences, even experiences that might be labeled as sexual. But Western society, and particularly American society, has been slow to recognize or conceptualize sexual experiences as a part of a child's development, an aspect of their lives worthy of study and discourse. As a result, neither the folk culture nor the scientific literature has had much to say on the subject. Parental discussion of child sexual behavior has not been commonplace, very little folk knowledge has been generated, age-appropriate sexuality education for children has rarely been initiated, and child sex research has not been encouraged, rewarded, or funded, except where the subject of child sexual abuse is concerned.

There have been improvements, however. There has been an explosion of studies of infant development and child development in the last three to four decades. Though these studies have not dealt with sexual development *per se*, they have added greatly to our understanding of child development. There have been a few studies of child sexual development and experience, a few K–12 sexuality education courses have been developed, and more than a dozen books of advice to parents on how to deal with the sexuality of their children have been written in the last ten years.

My own entry into the field of sexual science with an emphasis on child sexuality came about by accident. I had my degree in sociology and anthropology and was teaching courses in both at a liberal arts college. One of the courses I taught was on the sociology of the family, with the later addition of a course on sex and society. I required term papers of my students in both of these courses. Most papers I received were based on library research and dealt with subjects such as mate selection, marriage, divorce, reproduction, cross-cultural differences, etc. Enrollments were large in these courses, meaning that I read many papers. After a number of years of this routine, I introduced an alternate paper theme that literally changed my professional life. I suggested to students that they could choose to write on some aspect of their own life experience, which they would describe and analyze utilizing concepts introduced in the course. Many chose this new alternative. To my surprise, many wrote on some sexual experience that had occurred early in their lives. Given my traditional American background of little education about sexuality at home, in school, in college, or in graduate school, I was unprepared to critique such papers. It called for quick self-education. I read Moll, Freud, Ford and Beach, Kinsey, Money, and others. I attended summer institutes on sexuality, one being the first summer session offered by the Kinsey Institute. In subsequent years I spent two on-leave years in Sweden studying its sex culture and its touted sexuality education system; and I conducted studies of the sexual culture of several communities in Sweden and in the United States, in two Midwestern communities and in the urban-industrial Northeast. In this way I was accepted into the field of child sexual science, a field still only sparsely populated.

My goal in this book is to bring the reader up to date on what we know about early sexual development and sexual experience in the life of prepubescent children. I do so knowing full well the limits of empirical knowledge on child sexuality and the high emotion as well as the taboos that have hindered free, open, balanced discussion of the subject in the past. My hope is that this book will contribute to a freer and better informed atmosphere of discussion in the future.

The Sexual Life of Children

1

Early Development and Experience

Children are active and sensual, even before they are born. One of the earliest sensory systems of the human body to function is the skin, which begins to function during the embryonic stage of development.[1] The skin enables the organism to first experience its environment. The areas from which a response can be obtained are very generalized over the body. When the embryo is less than an inch long from crown to rump, and less than six weeks old, light stroking of the upper lip region or wings of the nose has been shown to cause a response, a bending of the neck and trunk. Stroking the palm of a fetus also results in a response. The conceptus in the womb is massaged with each movement of the mother as she carries on her daily activities. "In his dark, watery cradle of amniotic fluid, the fetus swims gracefully about, weightless, as buoyant and active as an astronaut on a spacewalk, capable of free-floating movement and reflexive action" (Rice 1975:61). Without this stimulation and activity, normal growth and maturation is hampered. Conceptus movement is even necessary for the development of bones and joints. Experience with prematurely born babies gives evidence of this. This effects of stroking, massaging, and rocking prematurely born babies who have missed the stimulating activity in the womb are dramatic, including a significant increase in body weight and nerve and body functioning.

The conceptus is active in the womb in response to pressure and touch from outside the mother's body. It responds to make itself comfortable in the womb. During the prenatal stage, the systems of the body do not operate in a fully automatic way; they need outside stimulation.

Some communication between the mother and the fetus is possible. One study involving two groups of mothers found that a group of mothers who touched and identified, through the body wall, the moving parts of the fetus and engaged in fetal massage increased the attachment between mother and newborn baby. Whether it was the fetus or the mother or both who were stimulated to an increased attachment is debatable.

The fetus in the womb also becomes acquainted with the outside environment because it can hear. Sounds within the amniotic sac have been recorded by inserting a small hydrophone in the mother's womb shortly before delivery. The mother's heartbeat and other organic sounds can be heard, but so can sounds from outside the mother's body. Conversations between the mother and others, at least their rhythm and tone, are clearly audible, and the difference between male and female voices can be detected. Other sounds, such as music played in the room, can also be heard clearly. The mother's voice will be the one the fetus most regularly hears, and if the rhythm, intensity, and timber of that voice provide a pleasant experience, the fetus at birth will be primed to like its mother.

Sucking activity and the grasping reflex are also present before birth. It is not uncommon to detect a fetus sucking thumb, fingers, or toes. The reflexive response that produces an erection in males has also been observed in male fetuses through ultrasound pictures as early as the seventeenth week of gestation. Because of analogies between the male and female genital systems, it is logical to assume that females develop the capacity for cyclical vaginal lubrication before birth as well.

In conclusion, the period before birth is a very busy and active one for the sensory development and experience of the human organism. For best development, the fetus must make the most of its experience in the womb.

After nine months in the womb the baby is born and enters the newborn phase of life. It is said that human offspring spend as much of their gestation period outside the womb as they have previously spent inside the womb because they are totally unable to care for themselves at birth. Because of its dependence, a baby must literally pass directly from the birth canal into the waiting, enveloping arms of the mother or other caretaker. The mouth is well developed for, and perhaps practiced in, sucking before birth, but the muscles and the limbs are not sufficiently developed for crawling or walking. The mouth is superior to the hand in direct activity and definiteness at birth. Its function in early infancy is fairly clear; that of the hand is uncertain. The food and protection needed must be immediately available at birth.

At birth, mother and baby become acquainted with one another. As any two people begin a new relationship, each is essentially unsettled, unfinished; that is, many aspects of selfhood remain unclarified, awaiting definition through the relationship. That is true for a baby and its mother; for the baby, nothing has been clarified. For the mother also, much remains to be clarified, especially if she is a first-time mother. Even if it is her second or subsequent child, the infant–mother relationship is unique in each case. Interaction that gradually, almost imperceptibly, becomes communication between them evolves slowly.

Let us look first at the mother's first minutes with her newborn infant. Klaus and Kennell (1976), who coined the term *maternal sensitivity*, give what appears to be almost magical powers to this meeting of mother and infant immediately upon birth. They see this sensitive period in the first minutes and hours after birth as very important for parent–infant attachment and as the wellspring for all the infant's subsequent attachments that will influence the quality of all future bonds. Recent research has cast doubt on the absolutely critical influence of these first minutes and hours. Nevertheless, the newborn is capable of beginning an attachment with the mother immediately upon birth. Under the best conditions, the mother's attachment to her baby appears to bloom during these first minutes and hours. After one month, Klaus and Kennell reported that mothers in a group of mothers who had immediate contact with their babies after birth were more reluctant to leave them with someone else, showed more soothing behavior when their babies cried and significantly more *en face* (the posture in which the mother rotates her face so that her eyes and those of her baby meet fully in the same vertical plane of rotation), and fondled their babies more than did mothers in a group with less initial contact with their newborns. Similar differences between the two groups of mothers appeared when the babies were one year of age. Just sixteen extra hours of contact within the first three days of life appeared to affect the behavior of the first group of mothers for one year and possibly longer. Mothers who had the early contact spent significantly more time in the *en face* position and in kissing their infants, whereas the other group of mothers often spent the time cleaning their infants. "The two groups appeared to focus on different ends of the baby. One group was busy cleaning whereas the other was giving love" (Klaus and Kennell 1976:63).

What capacities to relate does the newborn infant bring to the infant–parent relationship? The newborn's resources are meager indeed but only when compared with those of an adult. The infant's lack is especially clear when we consider that the greater the number of words in one's vocabulary, the greater one's ability to relate; the greater one's ability to take the role of another person, the greater one's ability to relate; the greater one's ability to play several roles, the greater one's ability to relate; the more one knows about one's self, the greater one's ability to relate. On all of these the newborn scores near the zero point. In other words, any relating a baby engages in with its mother shortly after birth is reflexive. The baby's initial movements are not socially acquired; they are physiological and psychological givens. So in the beginning the baby has its first experience with others in the enveloping arms of a parent, is at zero point as far as social development is concerned, and begins only with energy and some inborn predispositions, capacities, and needs.

To say that the baby at birth is totally incapable of fending for itself is not to say that it is only passive and receptive, however. From the moment of birth a baby has a relatively advanced sensory system. The first impulse appears to be the desire to establish contact with the outside world. A baby is born with a capacity for curiosity and an instinct to master—that is, to want to do what it is able to do, a basic psychobiological impulse or urge to experience and to control as large a segment of the outside world as is compatible with its locomotive limitations and limitation in the use of words. The healthy infant possesses an immediate desire to use each function and to perfect it as soon as it becomes physiologically possible. The whole body of impulse can be regarded as a yet undifferentiated desire for physical, emotional, and intellectual satisfaction. Those who observe newborns are struck with the active part—the initiative—that they show in the development of attachment to others. Observers point out that it is largely through the infant's own activity that attachment to the mother is effected rather than through stimulation by the mother or through her satisfying of the infant's creature comfort needs.

An attachment can be defined as a unique relationship between two people that is specific and endures through time. Maternal–infant attachment behaviors such as fondling, kissing, cuddling, and prolonged gazing are behaviors that serve both to maintain contact and to exhibit affection.

The newborn immediately begins to become actively involved in the process of communication. This is a first step in acquiring content (mentally) that he or she begins to share with others. This early communication is referred to as analogic communication—it is nonverbal and includes posture, gesture, facial expression, and voice inflection. In infant–parent interaction, communication must be analogic because the baby is not capable of digital language, which is verbal and includes words, signs, or symbols that carry meaning arbitrarily. In fact, infant–parent communication will be random rather than analogic on the infant's part and largely analogic on the parent's part because of the baby's inability to translate symbols into thought and action. The random and accidental gestures of the newborn baby may be attributed as communication by the parent even though the baby is not aware of communicating anything. The mother infers the baby's intentions from his or her behavior. The parent observes an action or an emotional state in the baby and makes a judgment as to its cause and intent. The parent is apt to attribute baby's behavior to some ability or intention rather than to external causes, and responds with behavior consistent with that interpretation. As the baby in turn internalizes the parent's responses and reacts to them, true communication begins to develop and the interaction becomes verbal and symbolic. The continual nonverbal and verbal statements that the parent and infant make to each other transform the two of them into interlinked intimates. Messages conveying intimate relationships can be verbal ("I love you") or nonverbal (e.g., an embrace).

Before a parent can act in other than a random manner toward the baby, the situation must be defined. It is the parent who patterns the baby's first random gestures into intimate and affectional responses, and baby soon begins to share with the parent an ability to generate an activity of a distinctly nonrandom kind that takes the form of meaningful actions interspersed with breaks. Baby begins to share with the parent its capacity to produce strings of meaningful actions. When these actions become interlinked and interdependent, as a result of repeated entraining over time, communication as such begins to take place.

There has been a surge of interest through the 1970s in the systematic study of infants in the presence of their mothers (Newson, 1977).Two behaviors have been found to be much more frequent among the mothers of secure infants than among the mothers of anxious, insecure infants. These behaviors are contingent pacing and encouragement of further interaction. A mother is identified as showing contingent pacing when she leans toward the baby, smiling and talking gently and in slow tempo, allowing the baby plenty of time to mobilize a response before she gives a gentle burst of stimulation. After little or no initial response from the baby, these mothers gently persist in stimulation, increasing positive responses as the infant becomes more responsive.

Between three and six months, the baby's smile becomes a smile of preference for the mother. The baby smiles more frequently for its mother than for others, and the smiles for her are bigger and more joyful. In contrast, mothers of anxious babies confine face-to-face interaction to routine care situations. They are initially silent with impassive facial expressions, and they are more frequently inappropriate in their pacing.

During the first minutes and hours after birth, the newborn is usually in a state of readiness to begin the attachment process. A newborn displays a number of different states of consciousness. The state most significant for attachment to begin appears to be a recurring quiet, alert state. In this state the newborn's eyes are wide open and able to respond to things in the environment. Initially, the newborn may be in this state for a period as short as a few minutes during the first hour after birth but may be in the state for as long as forty-five to sixty minutes. Even at this early age the newborn has visual preference and will turn its head in response to the spoken word. Having heard mother's voice as a fetus, the newly born baby appears curious to see what she looks like. Frequent recurrence of the alert state results from the interaction of a mother with her baby. If a newborn is in any state other than the alert state and its mother intervenes, it is likely that it will become alert. With favorable early attention and stimulation, newborns will track a triangle with their eyes on the day of their birth, can mimic the facial expressions of others before entering the first three- or four-hour postnatal deep sleep, and can vocalize within the first three days of life.

Eye-to-eye contact is an especially significant aspect of initial mother–newborn interaction since newborns lack meaningful vocal sounds. The distance between the eyes of the mother and the eyes of the infant when the mother is holding the baby in her arms is about twelve inches, the distance at which newborns can best focus on an object. A high degree of eye-to-eye contact between mother and infant has been observed to lead to immediate cessation of crying and a stronger bond with the mother. In observing the behavior of sixty-three first-time mothers and their newborns (age two to four days), onset of the newborn's vocalization was shown to be coactional rather than alternating, with the newborn joining in with the mother (Rosenthal 1982). The mother begins such vocalization rather than her vocalization being affected by the baby's preceding vocalization.

Human speech is not sound alone but also includes movement. Exchanges play a special role in the earliest human experience. Both the listening newborn and the mother move in time to the words of the mother, creating a type of dance. The newborn's motor behavior becomes entrained by and synchronized with the speech behavior of the mother. In fact, synchrony is an important element in mother–infant interaction. Microanalysis of these rudimentary infant–mother "dialogues" at birth shows that infants move synchronously with mother's speech as early as the first day of life. By this subtle entrainment of the baby's movements to the rhythm of the mother's speech, the baby gives the mother feedback that she can hardly resist. Their communication becomes a sort of "mating dance." Establishing mutual attention is often the first step in a whole series: mother may look where her baby is looking, may comment on what she sees, label it, and then in other ways verbally elaborate on it, thus beginning the pattern of communication.

Because of the newborn's dependency and immobility, first social experience (whether immediately on delivery or later) is almost of necessity within a two-person group, usually with the newborn's mother; the two-person group can be characterized as the true locus of intimacy. The two are not distracted by the presence of others. As they engage in intimate interaction with its high degree of emotional access, they are likely to develop pronounced feelings toward one another and to become jointly engaged in more and more activities. In other words, mother–infant pairs become developmental pairs. If one member (baby, for instance) undergoes developmental change, the other is also likely to do so. Hence not only reciprocal interaction takes place, but reciprocal development as well.

The earlier and more time mother and infant spend together, the more intimate the relationship becomes. In families in which maternal care is supplied by a single female, as contrasted with families in which caretaking is provided by more than one mother figure, mothers have been found to be more self-confident, less intellectualized in their relationships, more sensuous in their touching and handling of their babies, more likely to vocalize, more concerned with the well-being of their babies, more active, and more playful.

Interaction of family members with each other, and especially mother and baby, is both psychic and physical; the physical involvement is intense. Much of the early interaction is caregiving, and infant care that is not physically intimate is almost inconceivable. Physical handling that is gentle, firm, close, and frequent has a beneficial effect on the baby's attachment and responsiveness as well as on cognitive and motor development. Babies who have been held tenderly and carefully earlier tend later to respond positively to close bodily contact as well. It is the nonanxious parent who is most apt to hold her baby tenderly and carefully.

Intimate and sensate paired relationships can become so intense, consuming, and concentrated as to appear almost hypnotic and are sometimes referred to as hypnotic role taking. Activities involved in sucking at the breast for infants and coitus for adults fall into the category of hypnotic role taking. Ecstasy is another term used to characterize activity that is intense and perhaps erotic. In an ecstatic state a person is so carried away by the interaction that there is usually a suspension of voluntary action. Lewis (1965) reported having observed such ecstatic behavior in infants eight to ten months of age being held by their mothers. In a moment of apparent delight, the infant clasps the mother and begins rapid rotating pelvic thrusts at a frequency of about two per second and lasting ten to fifteen seconds.

Such thrusting behavior has also been observed in rhesus monkeys beginning as early as the eighth week of life. Thrusting behavior is most characteristic of adult coital behavior.

The most physiologically charged relations of infant and mother occur during breast-feeding as the two organisms mutually excite each other. Sucking at the breast is primarily a food-getting response for the baby, and unless the activity is eventually rewarded with nourishment, sucking gives way to fretting and crying. The reactions of older babies to breast-feeding shows signs of eagerness—rhythmic motions of hands, feet, fingers, and toes may occur along with the rhythm of sucking.

With an older baby there is more than just mouth–breast stimulation. The suckling infant puts its fingers into its mother's mouth; she responds by moving her lips on the baby's fingers. The baby moves its fingers; she responds with a smile. Babies also pat their mother's breast while sucking or during breaks in feeding, pat her face, turn a cheek to be kissed, clasp her around the neck, lay a cheek on hers, hug, bite. Such scenes can be observed in endless variation in any mother–child couple. In many cases the breast-feeding mother strokes and caresses her baby with the hand that is holding the baby and uses the free hand to prevent the breast from occluding the baby's nostrils. The sensuous enjoyment of nursing is likely to increase the baby's desire to suckle frequently and fully, thus also stimulating the secretion of milk.

Breast-feeding is a cooperative process. From the infant's side, problems may result from insufficient sucking, dislike of the nursing situation, and lack of responsiveness. Not all infants suck alike. Some fail to suck, some are weak suckers, some are normal, and some are active. However, sucking generally functions with a high degree of coordination from the first day and undergoes considerable improvement in subsequent weeks. The baby prefers sucking at the mother's breast to being bottle-fed.

The physiological responses to orgasm and to lactation are closely allied in nursing mothers. Uterine contractions occur during suckling and during sexual excitement. Nipple erection occurs during both. The observed increase in nipple length due to stimulation may lead to more effective sucking and even more stimulation for mother. The degree of milk ejection appears to be related to the degree of sexual response. Milk ejection for some nursing mothers has been observed to occur during sexual excitement with an adult partner as well as while nursing.

For some nursing mothers the nursing experience itself is sexually stimulating enough to carry them to the plateau level of sexual excitement and in some cases even to an orgasmic response (Kinsey et al. 1953; Masters and Johnson 1966). Some mothers experience serial orgasms and then drift into a refreshing slumber (Yates 1978). Regarding a baby's physiological-sexual responses to breast-feeding, babies possess a capacity for oral orgasm, a quivering of the lips and tongue in connection with breast-feeding followed by relaxation of the face into sleep. Oral orgasm can be frequent in occurrence during breast-feeding (Baker 1969). Baker observed that oral orgasm does appear to have a sharp peak similar to the genital orgasm following puberty.

Not only does the sucking experience give the infant pleasure, especially orally, but penile erections are also commonly observed in boy babies during the sucking experience. We must be cautious in attributing such genital response to stimulation resulting from the sucking experience. In other words, there may be organic pleasure, but the pleasure is not necessarily genitally sexual. It has been reported that vigorous sucking by active infants is accompanied by penile erections that may last throughout the sucking period and continue for several minutes after the breast is removed (Baliassnikova and Model, as reported in Halverson 1938; Newton and Newton 1967). On the other hand, Halverson (1938), as a result of his experiments on infant sucking, reported that though infants like to suck at the breast and prefer it to the bottle, penile erection never occurred during sucking at the breast. According to Halverson, so-called pleasure sucking activities have little or no connection with erection. So organic pleasure in infancy need not result in observable physiological-sexual reflex responses. Halverson did observe penile erections during feeding periods, sometimes as frequently as three or four times in a period, but he attributed these to occurrences in which infants encountered a difficult or irritating situation. He interpreted the erections as related to abdominal pressure, for when thwarting was introduced (such as removing the bottle or giving the infant a difficult nipple) the resulting movements were conspicuously characterized by severe contractions of the abdominal walls.

It is possible that Halverson's experimental situation itself served to deter the full pleasurable response since during the breast-feeding part of the experiment the infants reclined on the mother's lap while the mother leaned forward so that her breast was above the baby's mouth. To remove the nipple from the infant's mouth, the mother merely assumed an upright position. In other words, stimulation was severely limited to the presence of the nipple in the infant's mouth. No caressing, no fondling by the mother, no eye-to-eye contact, no opportunity for the infant to touch the mother's face, to place his fingers in her mouth apparently existed during the experiment. The question left unanswered is how many of these infant boys would have responded with penile erections under normal nursing conditions. The fact that marked abdominal pressure is probably the most effective stimulus bringing on penile erection does not rule out pleasant stimulation received in a normal nursing experience as a stimulant.

The sensory and sexual responses of infant and mother to their stimulating experiences appear to be almost wholly reflexive in nature; that is, they are neither planned nor intended. Masters and Johnson (1966) reported a heavy overlay of guilt expressed by some mothers who were sexually stimulated by the suckling process. Mothers sometimes cease breast-feeding in the fear that the experience may prove to be too sexually stimulating both for themselves and for the infant. Also, some mothers reject the opportunity to nurse a newborn because of high levels of eroticism experienced during the nursing of an earlier sibling. Winter (Lowry 1970) raised the issue of whether or not mothers who experience reflexive sexual pleasure during breast-feeding engage in erotic fantasy and found little evidence but did note a characteristic state of reverie, in which loosely connected pleasurable and charitable ideas replaced everyday constructive thinking during the sexual pleasure.

Not only do most mothers claim not to fantasize erotically when sexually stimulated during breast-feeding, they also do not generally attribute erotic motives to their baby, even to an infant son who has erections. Conn and Kanner (1940) asked parents whether erections had ever been noticed in their boys. Most mothers were surprisingly definite in asserting that they had or had not observed the phenomenon, yet sexual significance was not attached to it. Even mothers who displayed embarrassment when talking about any sex topic spoke freely about early erections in their boys, which would seem to indicate that they in no sense regarded infant male erections as sexual and certainly not as erotic.

Though mothers may not expect breast-feeding to be a sexual experience for them, they do accept that mother–infant interaction will be intimate. Society also expects it. In fact, if one were to design an infant socialization model intended to lead to the development of full erotic potential in a child, one could hardly improve on the model currently in vogue and recommended for the care of infants during the first year of life. If we look at infant care practices and the folk wisdom associated with them—especially the folk wisdom that has been influenced by the child development literature—we see recommendations to parents about the care of infants that would be expected to lead to the expression and enactment of what Freud described as incestuous desires. Infants are to be stimulated, cuddled, fondled, and aroused by the mother from the moment of birth. The relationship is often described in highly erotic terms yet without erotic intent. Fraiberg (1971) asked whether the relationship between mother and infant can be regarded as a love relationship. She suggested that it may not be a love relationship but that it will lead to love as mother and infant arouse in each other sensuous joy, conviction that they are absolutely indispensable to each other, and that life without each other is meaningless. Developmental studies suggest that infants' emotional maturation depends on such stimulation. As we pointed out, intimacy even at ecstatic and hypnotic levels is possible in physiologically and emotionally charged infant–parent interaction. Clinical studies credit insufficient physical contact between infant and mother as the cause of later inability to form attachments. It is suggested that if sexual identification is to develop in a child, attachment to parent must evoke and encourage corresponding responses from the infant.

Most activities associated with nurturing and hygienic care of babies is intimate and sensuous since it involves contact with sensitive organs—lips, mouth, anus, and genitals—that can produce in the infant a physiological response of a sensuous and sexual nature. These activities include (in addition to breast-feeding) toilet training, bathing, cleaning, and diapering. The highly physiological and emotionally charged first encounters of mother and infant play an indispensable part in the developmental process.

Part of the aim of tactile stimulation and close, warm, gentle, caring affirmation and intimate communication in infancy and childhood is to eroticize the child, to arouse, to awaken, to turn the child on to life. Part, but only part, of the eroticization process is the developmental process by which infants and children gain the necessary interest, knowledge, and experience to enable their sexual functioning to mature. The eroticization process is a process all children undergo, more or less successfully, determining whether the erotic activity in their lives will manifest its adaptive or its maladaptive potential. Becoming fully eroticized would involve optimal physiological, psychological, social, and cultural conditions, though it is rare that all of these are optimal at any stage in life.

Freud referred to the infant as polymorphous perverse, meaning that any infant has the potential for developing any type of erotic orientation. Erotic orientation is in large measure built on the person's physiological capacity to respond; cultural scripts help to guide and control its development. If we agree that the normal infant is born polymorphous perverse, then the process of civilizing the sexual potential that infants are born with consists of enhancing stimuli that are appropriate and desexualizing stimuli that might otherwise arouse the child in ways that are not considered good for the person or appropriate in society, at least in public. For example, in our society children are taught at an early age that touching the genitals or masturbating, if it is done, should be done only in private.

The very nature of childhood is itself socially constructed and is constructed at different times in different societies according to different models. What is called the protective model best characterizes the way children have been raised in recent generations in Western society and surely in the United States. The child is held "in trust" for a period in early life, a period of time in which it is believed that children must be protected and shielded from and kept ignorant of many aspects of adult life. This perspective on children, this method of child care, in addition to the spatial and age segregation that characterizes much of modern life, reduces the opportunity for children to develop an understanding of grown-up activities, thus contributing to their innocence and naiveté. Providing a good balance so as not to sexually over- or undereroticize a child is a challenge that many parents find awesome. There is a broad range of behavior that would be considered normal depending on the permissiveness of the society and the family as well as on the age of the child. Parents know, and need not regularly bring to consciousness, that the United States is not a society in which children are expected to be highly eroticized (Ford and Beach 1951). In the United States, sexually eroticized children are apt to be viewed as prematurely eroticized or distinctly pathological. Awakening sexually erotic interest performs functions, but it also creates problems, especially in a culture such as ours that believes that children should be sexually repressed. Unrestricted erotic gratification is seen as standing in the way of personality development, good interpersonal relations, and the operation of society.

The best recent study indicating how American parents feel about and deal with their children's sexuality is the interview study carried out by The Study Group of New York (Berges et al. 1983). Two hundred and twenty-five parents of children ages three to eleven from throughout the United States were interviewed. The sample is neither random nor representative since most of the respondents were middle-class suburban, but the researchers interviewed both men and women and sought persons of diverse philosophical positions.

Almost all of the parents were "enthusiastic and positive" about the value of touching—picking up, holding, hugging, fondling—as a way of expressing love, warmth, and trust and as "a method of reassuring children and helping to shape healthy and confident personalities" (Berges et al. 1983:66). Some parents admitted to darker and more complex emotions, being awed at the power of sensuality and feeling unable to reconcile themselves to its existence in children. Though they could not be certain at what point sensuous play became sensual play, many felt uneasy about confronting blatant sexual eroticism in their children.[2] Most seemed to think that children's pleasure in being touched—stroked, cuddled, rubbed, caressed—all over their bodies, even nongenital areas, was sensual even for the smallest toddlers. Many children let their parents know which areas of their bodies gave them special pleasure. Hence, though parents reported positive feelings about the overall value of physical contact, they believed that there would always be situations in which touching would have to be limited. Generally mothers were more comfortable with the sensual aspects of physical contact with their children than were fathers. Parents reported instances when their children attempted to touch them, rubbed against them in an innocent but erotic way or in a way that aroused them, asked to feel or play with the mother's breasts or nipples or to hug when in the nude. Parents expressed a great divergence of opinions on the touching of sexually sensitive areas of their children's bodies. Some said they would touch any part of a child's body unconditionally, while a much smaller number, especially fathers, described all sexual parts of their children's bodies as categorically and absolutely off limits for them. Often parental reaction to such touching had less to do with the nature of the touching experience than other considerations, such as the age or sex of the child and the context. As a general rule, parents seemed increasingly reluctant to touch the sexual parts of a child's body, whatever the reason, as the child grew older.

It has been the practice in our society, not only in sexual matters, to move children as rapidly as possible from a mode of interaction that includes touching, holding, and rocking to a mode of interaction that places the child at some distance, such as looking at, smiling at, vocalizing to. Children as young as four years of age are conscious of a nonreciprocating touching pattern developing as part of their tactile communication with their parents. That is, though their parents may be free to touch them, they are to be circumspect in their touching of their parents. Restrictions placed on contact through the maintenance of social distance provide a way in which awe can be generated and sustained. The blocked response becomes the essence of their emotional experience. Any response of a child to parental contact that alerts the parent to a growing sexual awareness in the child leads parents to reassess their policies and adjust their behavior accordingly. This is a way of letting the child know what types of affection, curiosity, or play are acceptable, including affection within the family circle. There were a number of parents (Berges et al. 1983) who said they placed no restrictions on the sexual forms of touching as long as the physical contact was of a positive nature—that is, not insensitive, aggressive, or dangerous.

Perhaps more children in our society are inadequately or undereroticized sexually than are highly or overeroticized. Though sexual development is in part a natural physiological process, unlike any other natural physiological process (such as breathing or the function of eliminating) sexual responsiveness is the most malleable and can be delayed indefinitely or functionally denied for a lifetime (Masters and Johnson 1970). The effect of delay can be observed even in young children. Spitz (1949) reported on infants in a foundling home wherein mother–infant interaction was nonexistent. The infants were raised without their mothers by an inadequate number of nurses—officially one nurse for eight infants, but in practice one nurse for ten or twelve. What was not provided was the tender, loving care so important to sexual development. Whereas almost all children reared in a normal family relationship play with their genitals within the first year of life, the foundling home infants did not play with their genitals even in their fourth year of life.

It was sexual nonfunction or dysfunction that led Masters and Johnson to develop a set of structured sexual experiences, the famous "sensate focus," to heighten awareness of the genitals of erotic and sensuous pleasure, for the socialization of some adult clients had made whole areas of sensuous experience taboo, especially making the genitalia a tabooed part of the body. According to the therapist Kaplan, again and again the history of patients who had sexual problems revealed that an extreme of punitive and moralistic attitudes prevailed in their families during childhood (Kaplan 1974). The parents provide inhibitory rather than excitatory attitudes and practices. They may be passing on to their child an erotophobia or aversion picked up in their own process of being socialized. The exclusion of the child from most aspects of family sexual life, broadly conceived so that the child is never touched tenderly and never sees the parents embrace or kiss, can conceivably lead to a form of affective deprivation, perhaps best described as sexual neglect.

A normal process of sexual eroticization would enable a child to learn, prepubertally, some of the attitudes and responses that will allow him or her to function appropriately as an adolescent and adult. Children who are sexually overeroticized for their age (there are some of these in U.S. society) are the product of an accelerated eroticization process. There is a danger that as a result they come to define themselves in sexual terms too early in life. As Freud (1938:592) stated it, "Seduction prematurely supplies the child with a sexual object at a time when the infantile sexual instinct does not yet evince any desire for it." In the words of Yates (1982:483), "the highly cathected focus on sexual learning seems to detract from social learning and a more even distribution of the libido."

Yates (1982, 1990) has found that for young sexually overeroticized children, the genitals may function as a central, organizing principle in their development as they seek, expect, and yearn for sexual experience. Their genitals become a well-differentiated part of the body and are highly valued, which contrasts markedly with the characteristically poor differentiation and undervaluing of the genitals among children generally in our society.Overeroticized children can be easily aroused through close contact with others—playmates, animals, adults. They may also have a problem in differentiating sexual from nonsexual touch. Sexual activity may come to be a permanent or exclusive mechanism by which they reduce tension. Preschool sexually overeroticized children are readily orgasmic and find sexual activity eminently pleasurable, so much so that it is difficult to find a comparable reward. Some form unusually intense, personalized relationships; others use sexuality as a way to make another child a friend, even briefly; some eroticize other children. Contrary to what Yates reported, Johnson (1991) stated that few such children, even those who participate in a full spectrum of sexual behavior with peers, report any real need or drive for sexual pleasure or orgasm.

Most of the sexually overeroticized children that come to attention, either through the courts or through therapy, are classified as sexually abused. They usually live in socially and psychologically disordered families, for so-called child sexual abuse in the family rarely occurs in isolation from high levels of familial distress and less than average educational and financial resources in the family. The consensus among child psychiatrists is that factors related to the makeup of families rather than the sexual behavior *per se* is the more pathogenic. A causal relationship between early parent–child sexual intimacy and emotional damage cannot be automatically assumed, nor do all sustain damage. Yates, who has worked with children sexually overeroticized in their families, stated categorically, "I believe that the eroticization process is independent of the emotional disturbances" (Yates 1982:483).

Besides abusive parents at the one end of the parent–child sexual relations continuum, parents at the other end of the continuum who think that withholding sexual expression is damaging sometimes exhibit a passion to instruct. Among them are persons who claim to practice family sexual expression in a highly educated, sophisticated, and carefully responsible manner. Such persons receive impetus from the writings of Rene Guyon (*The Ethics of Sexual Acts*, 1934) and others. The following cases are characteristic of such families.

> Their daughter was disturbed by her mother's agitation and breathing during intercourse. She otherwise seemed happy with being with her parents as they made love. Her mother explained the whole thing very carefully one day. Her daughter then said "I want to make love with you, mommy." At first her mother didn't know what to do and then

decided to go along as long as her daughter seemed OK. She put her hand on her daughter's genitals and suggested that her daughter put hers on top, showing her mother how it felt best. Her daughter started moving rhythmically and breathing heavily, exactly as she had seen her mother do. Her motion and breathing gradually built up to a climax and she relaxed. Whether she actually reached orgasm or mimicked it is uncertain. She was happy and thanked her mother. (Personal correspondence)

Daughter was about 3 years old. One morning she came in on her parents having intercourse. This was her first exposure to it and her parents could see she was confused and disturbed. As they described it, they "sent out good vibrations" making their enjoyment obvious. They included her in their lovemaking by holding her and talking with her. She responded positively and showed no further negative reactions then or later to her parents' lovemaking. (Personal correspondence)

A number of advocacy groups had some degree of notoriety in the United States during the 1960s and 1970s when there was interest in what was called child liberation. The Sexual Freedom League advocated sexual activity between children, but not transgenerational sex. The Rene Guyon Society advocated both child–child and child–adult sexual intimacy. One organization, Parents Liberation, apparently practiced familial sex and advocated child liberation in broad terms, and the Child Sensuality Circle was dedicated to the liberation of children in all aspects of life. None of these organizations grew to any national prominence, and today one hears little about children's sexual liberation. Rather, there has been a growing fear in our society that children are damaged through sexual contact of any kind.

In sum, there are children who receive the kind of tactile stimulation and close, warm, gentle, caring affirmation during infancy and childhood that promotes their sexual development in a manner appropriate to their age. At present there is no way of knowing how many children are raised in that way. Such infant and child care is in the middle range of what we call a sexual eroticization continuum. At one end of the eroticization continuum are those children who receive the greatest amount of public attention today, namely those who are sexually abused by being introduced into sexual experiences of a nature and intensity that is totally inappropriate for children, and sometimes of an insensitivity and brutality that can result in long-term physiological and psychological damage. At the other end of the continuum are children who, because of the lack of attention given them during their formative years or because of inhibiting factors in the family, grow up retarded in their sexual development or sexually undereroticized for their age. To care for infants and children in the tender, loving way regarded as appropriate in our society today is impossible without sexually eroticizing the child to some extent. The appropriate role for parents in the erotic sexual socialization of their children is a subject rarely discussed in our society.

NOTES

1. The term *conceptus* covers the lifespan of the human organism from conception to delivery. *Embryo* refers to the organism from conception to approximately the end of the eighth week of gestation. *Fetus* refers to the human organism from approximately the beginning of the ninth week to delivery.

2. Both the terms *sensuous* and *sensual* can be used to apply to any gratification of bodily desire or pleasure, but *sensual* commonly implies sexual appetite and refers, usually unfavorably, to the enjoyment experienced.

REFERENCES

Ainsworth, M. D. "Patterns of Attachment Behavior Shown by the Infant in Interaction with His Mother." *Merrill-Palmer Quarterly* 10(1964):51–58.

Baker, E. F. "A Further Study of Genital Anxiety in Nursing Mothers." *The Journal of Orgonomy* 3(1969):46–55.

Berges, E. T., S. Neiderbach, B. Rubin, E. F. Sharpe, and R. W. Tesler. *Children and Sex: The Parents Speak.* New York: Facts on File, 1983.

Blackman, M. "Pleasure and Touching: Their Significance in the Development of the Preschool Child—An Exploratory Study." In *Childhood and Sexuality: Proceedings of the International Symposium*, edited by J.-M. Samson, 175–202. Montreal: Editions Etudes Vivantes, 1980.

Bronfenbrenner, U. *The Ecology of Human Development.* Cambridge, Mass.: Harvard, 1979.

Carter-Jessup, L. "Promoting Maternal Attachment through Prenatal Intervention." *Maternal Child Nursing* 6(1981):107–12.

Cassel, Z. K. and L. W. Sander. "Neonatal Recognition Processes and Attachment: The Masking Experiment." Presented at the Society for Research in Child Development, Denver, 1975.

Clark-Stewart, K. A. "Interactions Between Others and Their Young Children: Characteristics and Consequences." *Monographs of the Society for Research in Child Development* 38(1973):1–108.

Condon, W. S. and L. W. Sander. "Neonate Movement Is Synchronized with Adult Speech: Interactional Participation and Language Acquisition." *Science* 183(1974):99–101.

Conn, J. H. and L. Kanner. "Spontaneous Erections in Early Childhood." *Journal of Pediatrics* 16(1940):337–40.

Dunn, J. B. and M.P.M. Richards. "Observations on the Developing Relationship between Mother and Baby in the Neonatal Period." In *Studies in Mother–Infant Interaction*, edited by H. R. Schaffer, 427–55. London: Academic Press, 1977.

Entwisle, D. R., S. G. Doering, and T. W. Reilly. "Sociopsychological Determinants of Women's Breast-Feeding Behavior: A Replication and Extension." *American Journal of Orthopsychiatry* 52(1982):244–60.

Field, T. N. "Discrimination and Imitation of Facial Expressions by Neonates." *Science* 218(1982):179–81.

Ford, C. S. and F. A. Beach. *Patterns of Sexual Behavior*. New York: Harper, 1951.

Fraiberg, S. "How a Baby Learns to Love." *Redbook*, May 1971.

Freud, S. *The Basic Writings of Sigmund Freud*. New York: Modern Library, 1938. (Translated and edited by A. A. Brill.)

Gagnon, J. H. "Sexuality and Sexual Learning in the Child." *Psychiatry* 28(1965):212–28.

Guyon, R. *The Ethics of Sexual Acts*. New York: Knopf, 1934. (Translated from the French by J. C. and I. Flugel.)

Halverson, H. M. "Infant Sucking and Tensional Behavior." *Journal of Genetic Psychology* 32(1938):365–430.

Johnson, T. C. "Understanding the Sexual Behaviors of Young Children." *SIECUS Report* 19(1991):12–15.

Kanner, L. "Infantile Sexuality." *Journal of Pediatrics* 4(1939):583–608.

Kaplan, H. S. *The New Sex Therapy*. New York: Brunner/Mazel, 1974.

Kinsey, A. C., W. B. Pomeroy, C. E. Martin, and P. Gebhard. *Sexual Behavior in the Human Female*. Philadelphia: W. B. Saunders, 1953.

Klaus, H. M. and J. H. Kennell. *Maternal-Infant Bonding*. St. Louis: C. V. Mosby, 1976.

Lennard, H. L. and A. Bernstein. *Patterns in Human Interaction*. San Francisco: Jossey-Bass, 1969.

Lewis, W. C. "Coital Movements in the First Year of Life: Earliest Anlage of Genital Love?" *International Journal of Psychoanalysis* 46(1965):372–74.

Lowry, T. P. "How Breast Feeding Arouses Women." *Journal of Sexology*, 37(1970):46–49.

Masters, W. H. and V. E. Johnson. *Human Sexual Inadequacy.* New York: Little, Brown, 1970.

Masters, W. H. and V. E. Johnson. *Human Sexual Response.* Boston: Little, Brown, 1966.

Newson, J. "An Intersubjective Approach to the Systematic Description of Mother–Infant Interaction." In *Studies in Mother–Infant Interaction,* edited by H. R. Schaffer, 47–61. London: Academic Press, 1977.

Newton, N. "The Role of Oxytocin Reflexes in Three Interpersonal Reproductive Acts: Coitus, Birth and Breastfeeding." *Clincal Psychoneurochronology in Reproduction, Proceedings of the Serono Symposia* 22(1978):411–17.

Newton, N. and M. Newton. "Psychologic Aspects of Lactation." *New England Journal of Medicine* 272(1967):1179–967.

Parsons, T. "The Incest Taboo in Relation to Social Structure and the Socialization of the Child." *British Journal of Sociology* 5(1954):101–17.

Rice, R. P. "Premature Infants Respond to Sensory Stimulation." *APA Monitor.* As reprinted in *Readings in Human Development,* 1976/1977 annual editions, 60–62, 1975.

Richard, J. "Child Sexuality." *RT-A Journal of Radical Therapy.*

Rorty, A. O. "Some Social Uses of the Forbidden." *Psychoanalytic Review* 58(1972):497–510.

Rosenthal, M. K. "Vocal Dialogues in the Neonatal Period." *Developmental Psychology* 18(1982):17–21.

Spitz, R. A. "Autoerotism: Some Empirical Findings and Hypotheses on Three of Its Manifestations in the First Year of Life." *The Psychoanalytic Study of the Child* III/IV(1949):85–120.

Yates, A. "Children Eroticized by Incest." *American Journal of Psychiatry* 139(1982):482–85.

Yates, A. "Eroticized Children." In *Handbook of Sexology VII: Childhood and Adolescent Sexology,* edited by M. E. Perry, 325–34. Amsterdam: Elsevier, 1990.

Yates, A. *Sex without Shame: Encouraging the Child's Healthy Sexual Development.* New York: William Morrow, 1978.

2

Self-Stimulation

During the first year of life infants discover and explore parts of their bodies. This early activity is more exploratory than autoerotic. Autoerotism is the technical term used to refer to self-gratification obtained through stimulation of one's own body, especially stimulation of one's genitals. By five or six months, many infants appear to enjoy pulling their ears or sticking their fingers in them. Some explore their genitals at this age as well. Levine (1957) reported that after six months infants gradually discontinue playing with their ears. Galenson and Roiphe (1974) reported that most boys began genital play at six or seven months of age, while most girls began at ten or eleven months. For their sample of infants, genital play among girls tended to disappear within a few weeks of onset, but boys continued casual play with additional visual and tactile exploration of the genitals starting at about eleven or twelve months of age.

An important distinction can be made between genital play and masturbation in infancy. Infants in the first year of life generally are not capable of the direct-volitional activity required for the behavior that we call masturbation. Any more or less random play with the genitals is nonspecific activity and should be labeled as genital play and not as masturbation. Genital play need not end with the end of infancy, as in the following case.

> There was physical pleasure to be derived from fondling my genitals. The satisfaction was enough to develop this practice into a habit.[1]

And touching or holding the genitals is not only associated with erotic pleasuring:

> Near the age of 6 or 7, holding the genitalia would give me a vague feeling of security. I would do this frequently in bed and it seemed almost an unconscious act that was associated with security.

According to Spitz and Wolf (1946), in the first eighteen months of life genital play is a reliable indicator of the adequacy or inadequacy of mothering. In their sample of cases, when the relationship between mother and infant was one in which the mother provided normal physical and emotional care and attention, genital play by the infant was present in all cases. When it was not provided, genital play was absent. This finding has been confirmed by others.

The greatest autoerotic satisfaction, and certainly the occurrence of orgasm, depends on manipulation of the genitals that is rhythmic and repeated. Rhythmic manipulation with the hand does not occur before a child is approximately two and a half to three years old, probably because small muscle control is not well developed before that. On the other hand, large muscle control is well developed and well coordinated as early as six months of age. Hence, some infants form a pattern of rocking that is rhythmic and repeated. They rock and bump their heads against the crib with vigor. Once they are able to sit up, additional types of rocking may be observed, all of which appear to bring satisfaction. Some sit and sway rhythmically, some lift the trunk and pelvis and bounce up and down off the surface on which they are sitting. Some do both by elevating themselves up and down and swaying to and fro, giving the appearance of rising as a person does when riding a trotting horse (Levine 1957). Elevating to hands and knees and rocking forward and backward appears to be the most frequent type of rocking and is not uncommon as early as six to twelve months of age. In other words, infants may discover the pleasure of rhythmic genital sensation through rocking before they have adequate hand and arm small-muscle control to masturbate. Rocking appears more satisfying than manual genital play in that infants in genital play can be easily distracted in contrast to infants who rock. Rockers often rock with great vigor and tension and are not easily distracted. The majority of rockers rock before going to sleep and immediately on rising. Many give it up before they are eighteen months to two years of age, but some continue to three years or older. One subject in Schaefer's (1964:128) interview study of thirty women reported that at age six she discovered that rocking and rubbing herself genitally on some bedclothes bunched between her legs could be continued "until something would happen—something moved, which I guess was a little orgasm."

Kinsey et al. (1948) reported that orgasm is not rare among children, both boys and girls, and has been observed in boys of every age from five months on and in an infant girl of four months. To understand the capacity of infants and small children to reach orgasm, we make a distinction between those who stimulate themselves and those who have been stimulated by others. Given the lack of capacity of infants for sustained rhythmic stimulation of their genitals, to determine the capacity of sexual response in infants would require stimulation by persons other than the infant. Kinsey had access to such data and reported on stimulation to orgasm of male infants under one year of age as follows:

> The behavior involves a series of physiologic changes, the development of rhythmic body movements with distinct penis throbs and pelvic thrusts, an obvious change in sensory capacities, a final tension of muscles, especially of the abdomen, hips, and back, a sudden release with convulsions, including rhythmic anal contractions—followed by the disappearance of all symptoms. A fretful babe quiets down under the initial sexual stimulation, is distracted from other activities, begins rhythmic pelvic thrusts, becomes tense as climax approaches, is thrown into convulsive action, often with violent arm and leg movements, sometimes with weeping at the moment of climax. After climax the child loses erection quickly and subsides into the calm and peace that typically follows adult orgasm. (Kinsey et al. 1948:177)

Kinsey and his colleagues have been castigated for not exposing the persons responsible for stimulating these infants to orgasm. Such behavior is generally regarded as child sexual abuse today.

Kinsey reported an increase in the percentage of individuals able to reach a sexual climax from 32 percent of boys two to twelve months of age to 57 percent of those two to five years of age and nearly 80 percent of preadolescent boys ten to thirteen years of age.

Masturbation has been largely ignored in books on infant and child development, yet it has long been recognized as a near-universal phenomenon. Roberts, Kline, and Gagnon (1978) found in a sample of American parents that 80 to 90 percent believed most children masturbate. Galenson and Roiphe (1974), utilizing interviews with parents for the first year and direct observation for the second year of life, found that for boys the onset of masturbation proper began at fifteen to sixteen months of age, whereas for girls a pattern of intermittent genital play was observed. Levine (1957) observed that most of the sexual activity at this young age remained genital play rather than true masturbation. He reported that most children, even through twenty-four to thirty months of age, indulge in genital play with a certain degree of satisfaction but in most cases without any apparent emotional excitement or increased stimulation. There appears to be a great deal of overlap between genital play and masturbation, however. Yates (1978) reports the following case of a seven-month-old girl.

> At about 7 months of age she took a great fancy to dolls. She would press her body against a large rag doll to which she was very attached and make rhythmic movements. The movements at first took place only in the evening at bedtime. At one year of age she and a doll became inseparable. She carried this doll about with her all day and from time to time would throw the doll on the floor, lie down on top of it, "as in the sexual act," according to her parents. Attempts to distract her during these episodes caused screaming. She would cling to the doll until she felt satisfied. The parents thought that she completed an orgasm in her own way. By about fifteen months of age the episodes had decreased in frequency and were of shorter duration and by seventeen months the masturbation took place only at bedtime.

From three years of age and on, children retain some memories of sexual experiences and can recall them. They may be able to report quite clearly on the first time they remember experiencing pleasurable genital sensation, the first time they masturbated, or the first time they had an orgasm. It may not in fact have been the first time, but earlier sexual experiences have been forgotten. The first memories that a child has appear to be those that were highly emotional.

According to Levine (1957), at three years of age most boys who masturbate do so manually by rubbing the penis or by wrapping the fingers around the erect penis and moving the hand. Still, at this age, many boys lie on their stomachs on a flat surface and writhe while engaged in other activity such as watching television. Some raise themselves slightly from the surface and propel themselves forward and backward, rubbing the genitals in so doing, and continue until orgasm is reached. A small number rub themselves against something—a hard pillow, the leg of a chair, a person's leg, or their own stiff forearm—and derive satisfaction in that way.

In girls, already at three years of age there are manifold varieties of masturbation (Kinsey et al. 1953; Levine 1957). These include thigh pressure; rubbing the genitals against a soft toy or blanket; manually stroking the labia and clitoris; and, less frequently, inserting objects in the vagina.

Some form of manual manipulation of the genitalia seems to be most common (Kinsey et al. 1953). Kinsey reports on a mother who observed her daughter masturbating.

> Lying face down on the bed, with her knees drawn up, she started rhythmic pelvic thrusts, about one second or less apart. The thrusts were primarily pelvic, with the legs tensed in a fixed position. The forward components of the thrust were in a smooth and perfect rhythm which was unbroken except for momentarily pauses during which the genitalia were readjusted against the doll on which they were pressed; the return from each thrust was convulsive, jerky. There were 44 thrusts in unbroken rhythm, a slight momentary pause, 87 thrusts followed by a slight momentary pause, then 10 thrusts, and then a cessation of all movement. There was marked concentration and intense breathing with abrupt jerks as orgasm approached. She was completely oblivious to everything during these later stages of the activity. Her eyes were glassy and fixed in a vacant stare. There was noticeable relief and relaxation after orgasm. A second series of reactions began two minutes later with series of 48, 18, and 57 thrusts, with slight momentary pauses between each series. With the mounting tensions there were audible gasps but immediately following the cessation of pelvic thrusts, there was complete relaxation and only desultory movements thereafter. (Kinsey et al. 1953:104–105)

Among the women interviewed by Schaefer, the earliest reported experience of first orgasm through self-stimulation was at age four. The subject discovered

> that pleasure involved in exposing my genital area to the forceful stream of water in the bathtub. My mother seemed to be very angry when she caught me doing this. . . . There was something very repressive about her when she reprimanded me—as though she was holding in something . . . but it was coming out in anger from her frozen face and stern eyes. (Schaefer 1964:127)

For many, even young children, masturbation is very satisfying from the first time they recall doing it.

> The first time I recall having a sexually pleasing sensation was when I was around 3 or 4. I remember feeling very proud of what I had learned (how to masturbate) and the strange sensation it aroused.

> I had no idea what I was doing or what it meant, but the feeling was terrific.

> The first time was a very unique, stimulating, and fascinating experience. I almost reached climax two or three times and then chickened out.

> I came across the enjoyable feeling by accident. The feeling was good, so I continued until I climaxed.

Three studies of female sexual activity contained data on the practice of self-stimulation in childhood and the number of subjects who attained climax by this means: in Davis's (1929) study, 25 percent to age ten had practiced self-stimulation and 12 percent had attained climax; in Kinsey et al.'s (1953) study, 19 percent practiced to age twelve and 12 percent attained climax; and in Schaefer's (1964) study, 43 percent practiced to age twelve and 23 percent attained climax. Among the Schaefer subjects, all those who reported self-stimulation before age twelve and who attained climax thereby continued the practice through adolescence and into adulthood whether or not they had been discovered or reprimanded. "For the ones who had not achieved orgasm, the pleasure evidently did not outweigh the guilt feelings and other negative pressures osmosed from the milieu" (Schaefer 1964:127).

Achieving orgasm can be a powerful motivator for girls as well as for boys.

> I *loved* it. I knew it was punishable . . . yet it was enjoyable, so I did it. It was comforting. (Schaefer 1964:204)

> Once having produced that kind of experience, it was imperative that I experience this, one way or another, each time. (Schaefer 1964:204)

But masturbating during childhood is not always viewed so positively.

> I remember trying my brother's "neat thing" but masturbation never thrilled me.

> I derived pleasure from a rather masochistic masturbation and my sex fantasies were sadistic.

> I cannot recall the exact date of my first masturbation or the circumstances leading to it, but I remember vividly the traumatic moments after I had completed the act. I didn't know what I had done or what had happened. Boy, was I scared!

I felt shameful about it.

I felt that somehow masturbation was going to stunt my growth.

I felt guilty about going to church the next morning.

Despite the pleasant feeling associated with orgasm, the words that women with masturbatory experiences used to describe the feeling attached to those experiences seemed to Schaefer (1964) to be guilt, anxiety, and shame. Kinsey et al. (1953) also noted that no other type of sexual activity had worried so many women as masturbation.

Masturbation was a good idea in the sense that it was a pleasure . . . but the guilt robbed it of all those good feelings, I think. (Schaefer 1964:205)

One subject was told by the teachers in her parochial school that "if you touch yourself in your private places, you'll go crazy" (Schaefer 1964:205).

In some cases a child fails to find masturbating satisfying because of failure to reach orgasm. The failure may be due to negative prior conditioning, ignorance due to lack of knowledge, or failure to discover a technique for effective self-stimulation.

At first I felt no satisfaction in it, but after a month of practice, I obtained my first orgasm.

In Scandinavia, where child sexual capacity is more widely recognized, preschool teachers, sex educators, and therapists have on occasion instructed children in better masturbatory techniques.

According to Thore Langfeldt (1990), the Norwegian sex therapist, those with serious masturbatory problems may need therapy to learn how to be orgasmic. He asserted that reducing anxiety, changing masturbatory techniques, and being supportive of sex in privacy are the most common effective aspects of the therapy, but that changing masturbatory patterns once they are established is very difficult in both boys and girls, even in small children as young as three to four years of age. Langfeldt reasoned that since girls have a less stereotypical masturbatory technique than boys, girls more often develop a masturbatory technique requiring a higher amount of genital stimulation than would be necessary with better technique.

The most satisfactory technique of genital self-stimulation, even for small children, appears to be repeated manipulation of a specific rhythmic form that leads to orgasm. According to Langfeldt, most children who masturbate to climax stop after one orgasm, but some children have several orgasms.

> By the age of 6, it had become a habit. I masturbated to orgasm at least once a day, usually at night. It was very pleasurable. It served the same purpose as a tranquilizer. I would almost immediately fall asleep and dream of my fantasies.

Not all children relax and go to sleep after reaching orgasm. A few appear to be stimulated by the activity. Levine reported on a three-year-old boy who would masturbate vigorously and end by sitting up alert, bright-eyed, and apparently satisfied and content. Masturbation is recognized as a tension reliever and is often observed among nursery school children. It is unquestionably increased during periods of emotional tension, but three-year-old children have also been observed to masturbate as an expression of delight and not when tired, stressed, or unhappy (Levine 1957).

A child's initial attempts at self-stimulation are inspired in a number of ways. Many discover the possibility of such activity entirely on their own and quite by accident. The great majority of females in the Kinsey et al. study (1953) learned to masturbate on their own as a result of their exploration of their genitals, but only 28 percent of the boys had discovered masturbation on their own. Most boys hear about it from others. Boys also learn by observing the behavior of other boys or through deliberate instruction given by one of their acquaintances.

> I began about the age 7. I believe it may have been when feeling a need to urinate. I began fingering my genitals and found it produced a very pleasurable sensation.

> It occurred when I climbed up a rope on a swing set. I discovered this quite by accident and told certain of my friends about it. They also proceeded to try.

> I started consciously masturbating at about age 6. I was hanging on a door by the knobs straddling the edge of the door. My penis rubbed on the door as I pulled myself up and down. It felt so good that I continued until I climaxed.

> The first time I remember masturbating was when I was about 10 years old. I discovered it while washing myself in the bathtub. I remember reaching orgasm.

> We were both young, prepuberty. We were out walking and stopped for a rest. After a prolonged rest, I noticed that he was masturbating. Finally, overcome by curiosity, I asked him to teach me how.

> I was about 8 or 9 and he was 9 months older. He encouraged me to try it and I did. I didn't enjoy it, but on his instruction to keep at it, I did achieve an orgasm.

> Once my younger sister asked what I was doing (masturbating) so I explained to her the feeling I got from it. She tried it and it felt good for her too.

> I happened upon my younger sister manipulating herself through her clothes. She showed me how to add pressure to the sides of my labia to gain a "funny feeling."

In the Kinsey sample, 9 percent of the boys had been masturbated by other males before they began to do it by themselves.

> My brother persuaded me to let him do something to me which he termed "jackin' off." I enjoyed the physical reaction which the act produced.

Similar same-age activity occurs among girls, but it is not nearly as common. Only about 3 percent of the females in the Kinsey et al. (1953) sample had begun masturbating as a result of childhood same-sex contacts.

> Several of us girls used to sleep together in a tent occasionally. We sometimes talked about sex, and under the guidance of one of the girls, we started to stroke each other's genitals and enjoyed the feeling. I wanted to see if I could reproduce those sensations by myself, and I could!!

Some girls wait months and even years after learning about masturbating before they try it themselves (Kinsey et al. 1953). Unlike girls, boys once they have heard about it rarely delay experimenting on their own.

As we have already mentioned, intense self-stimulation that occurs during the first year of life rarely involves use of the hands. Besides rocking, friction caused by rhythmic thigh pressure on the genitals is used. Thigh pressure is also used by older children wanting to avoid detection when masturbating.

Before the crushing boredom of a second grade classroom would grip me, I would swing my legs under my desk in a fashion which would end in an orgasm. I may have embarrassed a few teachers.

Masturbation is common during childhood, but by no means all children masturbate. We have no accurate count of the number who do or the frequency of occurrence for those who do. Several studies have dealt with the topic, but lack of methodological rigor and consistency makes comparisons between the findings of the various studies less useful than it might be. Sears, Maccoby, and Levine (1957) reported that only two fifths of the mothers said they had never noticed their children doing anything that could be referred to as masturbating. In a study involving 284 boys, Ramsey (1943) reported that 5 percent of those age six and under had had masturbatory experiences, and 10 percent of seven-year-olds had.

Some children of both sexes masturbate in early childhood. Reports conflict as to which sex has the higher incidence. Kinsey et al. (1953) reported more girls than boys. Ramsey (1943) summarized five personal-interview studies that, when taken along with his own study, indicate that masturbation occurs at some time in the sexual histories of nearly all males. In Ramsey's sample, three fourths reported that their first experience was between the ages of ten and sixteen. Fourteen percent of those eight years old reported masturbatory experiences, 23 percent of those nine years old, 29 percent of those ten years old, 52 percent of those eleven years old, 73 percent of those twelve years old, 85 percent of those thirteen years old, 95 percent of those fourteen years old, and 98 percent of those fifteen years old. The highest percentage increment came at ages eleven, twelve, thirteen, and fourteen, and in that order. The increase at each age from six to age fifteen was 5.3, 4.2, 4.6, 8.8, 5.9, 24.7 (age eleven), 19.1, 12.2, 10.2, and 3.1. Note the marked increment between age ten and age eleven. This is a considerably more rapid rise in incidence than that reported for a British sample (Capes 1972) and perhaps for a Norwegian study (Langfeldt 1990) as well, but both Capes's and Langfeldt's data agree with Ramsey's that by the end of puberty masturbation is almost universal among boys.

We do not have incidence data for girls that are comparable to the Ramsey data for boys, but it has been generally observed that the incidence of recalled onset of masturbation is a smaller percentage for females than for males at each age. In the Kinsey et al. sample (1953), 4 percent of females reported remembering having masturbated at age five; 7 percent at age seven; 13 percent at age ten; 19 percent at age twelve; and 28 percent at age fifteen. Langfeldt (1990) reported a considerably higher percentage for fifteen- to sixteen-year-old Norwegian girls; Langfeldt reported an incidence of about 50 percent masturbating to orgasm. The difference between Kinsey's and Langfeldt's findings could reflect, besides sampling differences, differences in culture and in time. Langfeldt's data were collected almost forty years after Kinsey's.

As to the frequency of masturbating for those with masturbatory experience, Ramsey (1943) reported a wide variation in frequency of occurrence for the 257 boys with experience, from a single experience to a maximum frequency of over 1,000 times per year. Seventy-three percent of the boys reported masturbatory frequencies of one to four times per week. Nor are such frequencies uncommon for girls, though there are less girls who masturbate.

As to the effect of masturbation, masturbation appears to be a common experience in normal and healthy infants and children. Levine (1957) reported that, except for excoriated penile shafts and irritated vulvae and perineum in some children, "most of the active masturbators that I have observed have been beautifully built with good posture and excellent muscle tone" (Levine 1957:123). Evidence of guilt feelings in children who masturbate is relatively common in our society.

> It has always puzzled me as to exactly where I got the feelings of guilt. As far as I can remember, my parents never said much of anything about sex. Certainly nothing that would lead me to believe sex was wrong or bad. Possibly it was because they said nothing that I felt there was something secret about sex. Likewise, I can't remember picking up much in church that would have led me to believe that I should not masturbate. Maybe I merely picked up the guilt feelings about sex from off-hand comments I might have heard. At any rate, regardless of where I acquired my feelings, I definitely felt it was wrong to masturbate and had deep guilt feelings about the activity.

The Child Study Association, in its 1969 publication *When Children Ask About Sex*, referred to masturbation as a necessary phase of sex maturing and suggested that it helps parents to think of masturbation as part of the growing-up process instead of as a dangerous habit. This perspective has been around for some time, yet parents find it a perspective difficult to accept when their own children are concerned. If children could remember the kind of sexual socialization they had received in childhood, they would likely know why they feel guilty when masturbating.

Several recent studies (Berges et al. 1983; Gagnon 1985) have dealt with the topic of parental awareness of and reaction to child masturbation. Gagnon found that a large majority of parents, especially mothers, recognize that children do masturbate; a smaller number, but still a majority, agreed that masturbation was all right, especially mothers of sons, 60 percent of whom thought it was all right. A large number of parents reported that they had observed their children masturbating (Berges et al. 1983). Levine (1957) reported that almost 100 percent, if not 100 percent, of all parents that he had questioned or observed expressed some revulsion when watching their children masturbate, even if they made no attempt to stop it. Berges et al. (1983) found that parents took great satisfaction in observing their children's enjoyment of the various parts of their bodies—except when it came to genital touching, even though they acknowledged that their children derived pleasure from it. Gagnon (1985), too, found that only a few parents actually approved of their own child masturbating, mainly mothers of sons and only 4 percent of them. The most common reaction was to ignore the child's masturbating or to suggest that the child do it in private. A fourth of the mothers told their daughters that masturbating was harmful for them; less than 10 percent told their sons the same thing. Less than half of the parents wanted their children in adolescence to have a positive attitude toward masturbation; 62.5 percent of mothers with liberal sex attitudes wanted their sons to have positive attitudes. According to Berges et al. (1983), a sizable group of parents saw masturbation as a positive part of human development, a good thing in itself, a joyous and enriching experience. It is a rare mother who is as positive when it concerns her own child as the mother of the boy in the following case.

> My mother asked me straight out if I masturbated. I didn't want to discuss it, but I said that I did. My mother's only reply was that she didn't want me to masturbate for short periods of time because I could become a premature ejaculator.

There is little doubt that the attitudes of parents influence the attitudes of children toward masturbation.

> The openness toward nudity in my family created an atmosphere where I was not self-conscious or reluctant to acknowledge my genitals. Consequently, I started masturbating at a very young age. I had no negative feelings about it.

Parents in the Berges study indicated rather apologetically that they had never brought up the subject of orgasm with their children. The majority did not think their children had any understanding of what orgasm was.

Masturbation is not a topic commonly discussed in sex education material prepared for parents of young children in our society (Martinson 1992).

NOTE

1. All cases of sexual experiences used in the text are from the author's files unless otherwise indicated and are drawn from over 200 cases of recall of childhood sexual experiences by undergraduate college students. Cases are used to elaborate on a point, not to prove it.

REFERENCES

Berges, E. T., S. Neiderbach, B. Rubin, E. F. Sharpe, and R. W. Tesler. *Children and Sex: The Parents Speak.* New York: Facts on File, 1983.

Capes, M. "Sexual Development in Childhood and Its Problems." *British Medical Journal* 4(1972):38–39.

Davis, Katherine B. *Factors in the Sex Life of Twenty-Two Hundred Women.* New York: Harper and Bros., 1929.

Gagnon, J. H. "Attitudes and Responses of Parents to Pre-Adolescent Masturbation." *Archives of Sexual Behavior* 14(1985):451–66.

Galenson, E. and H. Roiphe. "The Emergence of Genital Awareness during the Second Year of Life." In *Sex Differences in Behavior*, edited by R. C. Friedman, 223–31. New York: Wiley, 1974.

Kinsey, A. C., W. B. Pomeroy, and C. E. Martin. *Sexual Behavior in the Human Male.* Philadelphia: Saunders, 1948.

Kinsey, A. C., W. B. Pomeroy, C. E. Martin and P. H. Gebhard. *Sexual Behavior in the Human Female.* Philadelphia: W. B. Saunders, 1953.

Langfeldt, T. "Early Childhood and Juvenile Sexuality, Development and Problems." In *Handbook of Sexuality VII: Childhood and Adolescent Sexology*, edited by M. E. Perry, 179–200. Amsterdam: Elsevier, 1990.

Levine, M. I. "Pediatric Observations on Masturbation in Children." *Psychoanalytic Study of the Child* 6(1957):117–24.

Martinson, F. M. "Child Sexual Development and Experience: What the Experts Are Telling Parents." Paper presented at the Society for the Scientific Study of Sex annual meeting, November 1992.

Ramsey, G. V. "The Sexual Development of Boys." *American Journal of Psychology* 56(1943):217–33.

Roberts, E. J., D. Kline, and J. Gagnon. *Family Life and Sexual Learning. A Study of the Role of Parents in the Sexual Learning of Children.* Cambridge, Mass.: Population Education Inc., 1978.

Schaefer, Leah C. *Sexual Experiences and Reactions of a Group of Thirty Women as Told to a Female Psychotherapist.* Report of an Ed.D. doctoral project. Columbia University, 1964.

Sears, R. R., E. E. Maccoby, and H. Levine. *Patterns of Child Rearing.* Evanston, Ill.: Row, Peterson, 1957.

Spitz, R. A. and K. W. Wolf. "Anaclitic Depression." *Psychoanalytic Study of the Child* 2(1946):313–42.

Yates, A. *Sex without Shame: Encouraging a Child's Sexual Development.* New York: William Morrow, 1978.

3

Sex Play in Childhood and Preadolescence

The term *child sex play* is usually used to refer to that part of young children's intimate play life wherein children mutually engage in activities that adults designate as sexual, play such as exposing themselves to each other and touching each other's genitals. The term *child sex play* can be broadened to include any type of same- or opposite-sex sexual activity involving two or more children of the same age that occurs at any time prior to the onset of adolescence.[1]

Infants before they are old enough to walk or even to crawl show interest in others of their age by actively seeking eye and touch contact with each other. And they have more contact with others at this age than one might expect. Many infants, even as young as six to twelve months old, have contact with other infants. When in each other's presence, infants watch each other, point at each other, and move toward each other. When within reaching distance, they may touch each other on the face, body, or clothing and then engage in games of mutual pointing and touching. The relatively high frequency of watching, pointing, touching, as well as vocalizing in the presence of another infant suggests a strong interest in peers even at this early age. Because of their lack of touch finesse and lack of familiarity with such an exchange, the game may end in one or both indicating a desire to be rescued from it.

Whereas infants have a very limited mobility, young children are able to walk about and to play with peers under less care and supervision. This extends the range and increases the variety of peer contact and experiences, including some experiences that adults characterize as sexual. Playing with siblings and neighborhood children, attending kindergarten, and beginning grade school open many new possibilities for interaction. As young children learn to play together in an amicable fashion, they single out one or two playmates for whom they show real affection. Freud (1938) observed that children from three to five years old are capable of evincing a very strong object selection that is accompanied by strong affect. But it can occur even earlier. Kinsey's interviews with a small sample of two-year-olds and their mothers revealed a good deal of cuddling and kissing by two-year-olds (both boys and girls) not only of their parents but also of others. Reporting on life in the Israeli *kevutza*, Spiro (1958) noted in a bisexual children's peer group with a mean age of two that the most frequent expression of heterosexual behavior consisted of a simple embrace of one child by another, followed in frequency by stroking and caressing, kissing, and touching of genitals. Bell (1902), in his study of more than 2,500 cases of affectionate friendships between three- to eight-year-olds, found what he called the emotion of sex-love beginning in the behavior of children in the third year of life. This emotion was exhibited in paired relationships through such activities as hugging, kissing, lifting each other, scuffling, sitting close to each other, confessing to each other and excluding others, grieving at being separated, giving gifts, extending courtesies to each other that are withheld from others, making sacrifices such as giving up desired things or forgoing pleasures, and being jealous. Bell characterized the love demonstration of children as spontaneous, profuse, and unrestrained. The following case is illustrative.

> At the tender age of 5, I found the idea of a boyfriend very appealing. We experimented with kissing on several occasions; however the idea formed, we were sure we were in love. When I was 7 or 8, he asked me to marry him. I was overjoyed and really believed that we would marry when we "grew up."

> I, a girl, was about 5 years old and never played with other girls. Children in the neighborhood looked upon us as an "engaged couple." One afternoon while playing in his house we decided to take off our trousers. There was something exciting about it, something I had never felt before.

> Kindergarten was curiously arousing in that I enjoyed sleeping next to girls on our mats during rest periods.

Since adults are reluctant to inform about or to model sex behavior for children, children make their own attempts at satisfying their curiosity about sexuality and sex life. This results in bodily exploration, sexual experiments, and sexual games carried on largely in secret from adults. Hence, children live out their unorganized affectional and sexual feelings and their curiosity through their play. Their interest in their own genitals and the genitals of their peers increases. They study their own genitalia, fondle them, and show them to others. Gundersen et al. (1981) found in a nursery school that boys' interest in the genitals of others was primarily directed toward interest in the genitals of other boys; girls also showed a marked interest in boys' genitals. In other words, both sexes were preoccupied with boys' sexual organs. Discovery of boys' genitals excites more interest; not only is there more to see, so far as external genitalia is concerned, but an unexpected erection adds to the excitement.

> When we played with each other in the nude my penis became erect; I marveled at this. She asked what it was for. I didn't know.

Doctor/nurse/patient games, family role-playing games, and similar forms of play are common children's play.

> It was at the age of 5 that I, along with my three friends who were sisters and lived next door, first viewed the genitals of a boy. They had a male cousin who came to visit and we all ended up behind the furnace playing doctor. No matter what he would say his symptoms were, we were so fascinated with his penis that it was always the center of our examinations. I remember giggling as I punched it and as I dunked it in some red food-colored water that we were using for medicine. This seemed to give him great enjoyment. One girl put hand lotion and a bandage on his penis and in the process he had an erection. We asked him to do it again but their was no such luck. He suddenly felt embarrassed and offended and said he didn't want to play anymore.

Undressing and thereby exposing one's body to a playmate is surely one of the earliest and least organized forms of young children's sex play. It is spontaneous, light-hearted, and exploratory rather than goal oriented. They are not sure what they are looking for or what they will find. They may act excited, giggle, and feel and act silly. It is not sexuality that excites them as much as the discovery of something new or the feeling, due to previous conditioning, that they are doing something naughty. Young children are fascinated by undressing and exploring each other, even in societies where nudity of children is more readily accepted than it is in the United States. Gundersen et al. (1981) reported that being naked in itself appeared to be very enjoyable for Norwegian nursery children, and there seemed to be very little shyness when playing outdoors or indoors, although some children never undressed. Generally the teachers did not interfere when children undressed.

Young boys are often disappointed the first time they see girls' genitals, in that they expect more.

> I was very disappointed at what I saw, for there was only a slit and nothing more.

It is not uncommon for child care staff to report "sex epidemics" occurring among children, especially in spring when the children wear less warm, protective clothing, wear more sundresses and shorts, and show a renewed interest in each other's bodies, how they work, and what they look like. Even play as intimate as penis kissing and vagina kissing is reported by child care staff.

Bodily exploration among friends is a popular game among four-year-olds in day care. Such play is more pronounced if the children in the nursery do not have activities planned for them. Their sex play tends to go in fits and starts. Hagerfors, speaking about sex activity in a Swedish nursery, complained that the children sometimes closed themselves in the private area, an area provided for children in Swedish nurseries, engaged in sex play, and talked only about sex. The staff told the parents what was going on but otherwise played no part in it except to say something like, "Stop harping on that, now we are going to do something else; we don't want to hear any more about penises." Scandinavian children generally are more sexually knowledgeable than American children; they are not necessarily more or less likely to engage in sex play, but the type of play reflects their greater knowledge. That young children are sexual and can be expected to engage in some sexual activity is more accepted in Scandinavia than in the United States.

At age five children begin to be more self-contained, serious about themselves, and impressed with their ability to initiate grown-up behavior. Sex play and games involving exposure are likely to decrease in frequency as children become more modest and less apt to expose themselves. There is less bathroom play and interest in bathrooms than occurs earlier. They are familiar with, but less interested in, the physical differences between the sexes.

Youth who remember childhood sexual experiences often remember them because of something noteworthy that happened—and that is often the reaction of a parent, as in the following.

> Out of curiosity she and I, about age 5, exposed our genitals to each other. We were caught in the act. Mother sent her home, told me not to ever do that again, gave me a good licking and sent me to my bedroom for the rest of the day. I couldn't understand why she was so mad; she never explained to me why I was punished. I was hurt and confused and, worse yet, my curiosity was still not appeased. This event is solidly implanted in my mind, for it was the first time I had encountered such fury from my mother.

Even when no physical punishment results, it can happen that one of the children's parents will enter the room "hollering and screaming," as one boy reported. On the other hand, the following case of an understanding parent seems to be more typical of parental responses today.

> My mother told me that she had found out that a neighbor girl and I had been exposing and touching each other's genitals in the closet. She did not scold me but told me that it is natural that children are curious and want to know what the opposite sex looks like. I felt relieved, having believed that I had trodden on forbidden ground.

Nor do both parents necessarily agree on the seriousness of children exposing themselves to each other.

> I still remember how much I liked my father. Mother told him what I had done. He wasn't angry at all, just talked to me calmly, and tried to get me to stop crying. I don't think mother ever understood how much she hurt me psychically that time.

Preadolescence is the span of four or so years of childhood immediately preceding adolescence, though the onset of adolescence is somewhat variable. Interest in sex is quite high in preadolescence, though sex exploration and sex play may be less common than in earlier childhood. Preadolescents are more cognizant of and influenced by the sexual scripts and social taboos subscribed to and taught by adults they are in contact with than are younger children. Preadolescent boys and girls are conscious of gender differences and play a great deal as separate gender groups. Girls, in preadolescence, play with dolls and paper dolls, play house, and stress more complex adult relationships than they did at earlier years, while boys are more physically active and object oriented.

Cross-sex antagonisms develop that are in part due to these and other differences, in part due to the effort of individuals in each gender group to identify more closely with their own sex and separate themselves from the other sex. Individuals also become aware of differences that adults instill in each sex. Sex differences—innate and those imposed by adults—become incorporated into boys' and girls' subcultures. The male subculture supports and encourages sexual activity; this affects the incidence of their sexual experiences. How much the incidence of sexual experience is affected by sociocultural and how much by physiological factors is a moot question and impossible to ascertain. We do know that penile erections come quickly and easily in preadolescent boys, more quickly than in adult males, though the speed at which orgasmic climax is reached in sex play varies widely as it does in adult males. The capacity of preadolescent boys to achieve repeated orgasms in limited time exceeds the capacity of teenage boys, which in turn exceeds that of adult males (Kinsey et al. 1948).

Ramsey (1943), in studying the erotic responsiveness of nearly 300 boys from an urban junior high school in a middle-sized Midwestern city (the respondents were mostly white, middle class, and Protestant), asked each boy to rate his response to each item on a list of erotic stimuli. Ramsey found wide variation in the erotic responsiveness of each boy. The items, arranged in declining order based on the item's rating as a stimulant by the group as a whole, were as follows: sex conversation, female nudity, obscene motion pictures, and daydreaming. About 50 percent of the boys reported erections resulting from some type of nonerotic stimulus. The situation in which responses occurred usually involved elements of fear, excitement, or other emotional stimulant. The items reported as nonerotic stimuli included carnival rides, war motion pictures, being late to school, reciting before a class, fast rides, playing a musical solo, band music, and fear of punishment. These responses were most frequently reported for boys aged ten, eleven, and twelve years.

For girls the incidence of preadolescent heterosexual sex play (i.e., the active incidence) appears to be highest in the younger years of preadolescence rather than in the older years of preadolescence. Eight percent of the females in the Kinsey et al. (1953) sample recalled heterosexual sex play at ages five and seven, but fewer recalled it in the years of preadolescence. Only 3 percent recalled having sex play just before pubescence. For most, preadolescent play was restricted to a single experience or to a few stray experiences. Exceedingly few of the girls seemed to have developed a pattern of frequent or regular sexual activity. The situation was different for boys. Seven boys for every one girl were engaging in heterosexual play as they approached adolescence; the girls who did accept contacts at that age apparently had more than one male partner (Kinsey et al. 1953).

Neither Ramsey (1943) nor Kinsey et al. (1953) show evidence of a striking increase in the incidence of sex activity as puberty is reached. Kinsey's data on the active incidence for each year did show that for boys who later go to college, heterosexual play of all kinds dropped off after about age ten, presumably in response to a redefinition of the meaning of this type of behavior. But among boys who did not finish high school, there was reportedly a high level of continuity of heterosexual activity throughout preadolescence and into adolescence. There were gender differences, however. Among males a much higher percentage carried their preadolescent play directly into their adolescent and adult activity than was true of females. The discontinuities between the adolescent and preadolescent activities of the female appear to be the product of social custom and not of anything in the female's biological or psychological makeup. The incidence of heterosexual sex play for girls just prior to puberty in part depends on restraints placed on them by their parents as they approach puberty—restraints that girls often resent after a carefree childhood.

Many naive and more or less erotic experiences of childhood carry over and are elaborated on in preadolescence, for it is early preadolescence before some children get around to the stage that often occurs much earlier, namely exposing themselves to each other. At this older age the game of exposing is not always as innocent as is exposing at younger ages.

> She often let me watch her urinate, but I always refused to permit her to watch me. I repeatedly told her that I was "different." Later that year I became bolder. She and I ran back into the woods and undressed in front of each other. I suggested that we touch each other's genitals, but she refused.
>
> When we were in the fort, the boys asked us to "take down our pants" so that they could see what we looked like and they in turn would do the same. My friend and I didn't go for the idea but after lots of friendly persuasion we agreed to do it on the condition that everyone was sworn to secrecy. We all really gawked after the pants were down and I remember being rather embarrassed but also fascinated at looking at the different penises. This was not my first time seeing a penis because I had watched my dad get dressed. I recall that some of the boys would sometimes have erections and one boy told another that he really had a "boner," having an erection with the largest penis of all the boys.
>
> He told me to pull down my pants and he did the same. He had an erection and he put his penis between my legs. He said that this was how to "fuck." Being totally unfamiliar with the term and his not

knowing the exact technique, I thought it was a silly thing to do and never attached much importance to the incident. I often wonder what would have happened if he actually knew what to do. I guess I must have been a permissive, ignorant child.

To play our game it was necessary that we both take down our pants and expose our genitalia. The leader of the game had a nickel, which he was ready to toss. If I called the correct side of the coin as he tossed it, he would then touch his erect penis to my genitals. It was like a gentle love pat, not a forceful shove. After the first few times, no matter which side of the coin landed up we touched our genitals every time. I remember experiencing great pleasure when his penis touched my genitals. It was a tingly feeling that surged through me. I liked the feeling and thus we engaged in the game about 15 times that afternoon.

My friend and I decided to organize a club. Right away we recruited a third member, a girl. Our intentions were to hold secret meetings for the purpose of displaying our naked bodies to each other. We were quite excited about the potential of our group, especially since we anticipated the further physical development of our most important member, the girl. We realized that we were doing something not quite proper and this realization was reflected in the name we selected for the club, "The Naughty Club." Our girl member moved away before our club could achieve its objectives. When she moved away we decided not to hold any more meetings.

The first time I recall ever thinking about "sex" or boys having to do with sex was when I was about 11 years old when still within the context of my childhood group. We would have secret meetings in my playhouse, burn candles, and pass around "dirty" pictures that we had cut out of magazines. One time we even got the idea of pulling down our pants in front of each other. This was never repeated, partly because I objected to it so violently and partly because we lost fascination with these meetings after a while.

Based on participant observation in four elementary schools, Thorne and Luria (1986) analyzed relationships between sexuality and gender in the experiences of nine- to eleven-year-old children. They found, as have other researchers, that gender segregation—the separation of girls and boys in friendship and casual encounters—is central to daily life in elementary school. It is so common that they found it meaningful to speak of separate boys' and girls' worlds. Girls tend to focus on themes of romance in their conversations about sexuality; boys focus more on sex. Crushes and hero worship that occur among young children also occur among preadolescents.

> Through grade school and into junior high I had "crushes" on older boys, boys 6–7 years older. It would actually hurt me to see them with other girls. You don't have to be very old to be hurt; it starts at a very tender age.

> We got terrible crushes on boys. You'd think the world would end if one of these nights you wouldn't receive a call.

> During the summer I and a couple of my friends developed crushes on a couple of girls, and that summer was spent in a sort of competition as to who would be the first to "establish communication" and ask their girl on a date. It was an especially confusing period of time for me, because I was experiencing feelings that I hadn't felt before. I'm sure some of the things I said and did were rather foolish, but it was perfectly serious.

> At the age of ten, sexual topics started to become the main area of conversation, both at the lunch table and on the playground. Through grade school there was always mention of the subject, especially in jokes, but it seemed to be stepped up, I suppose in response to obvious physical changes that were occurring in both us boys and more prominently the girls.

Though they are interested in romance, girls are not all equally accepting of their "more prominent physical changes," as demonstrated in the following two cases.

> One morning in the fifth grade I noticed humps appearing on my chest. I was amazed, scared, and pleased all at the same time. To show how pleased I was, I called all of my girlfriends' attention to this phenomenon and let them "feel" my breasts.

> The girls in our school were ridiculed to a certain degree by the others if they had a bust. I very much did not want to be singled out and made fun of, so I tried very hard to hide my changing figure. When my mother bought me a bra while I was in the sixth grade, I refused to wear it. Instead I wore two undershirts and a tight slip to hide my bust.

Much same-sex as well as cross-sex play in preadolescence has nothing to do with sex. The play of boys is more active and vigorous than is that of girls, but even boy–girl play is apt to be active and vigorous; to succeed at such play girls must adopt some of the active, vigorous play patterns of boys. In recent generations, gender differences have not been as rigidly defined and girls and boys overlap in many characteristics, such as style of dress, sports, and social activities. Boy–girl play at this age contains many approach and avoidance routines, as both sexes are practicing new roles. It is not always clear to an adult observer whether they are fighting with each other or attempting to establish a relationship. Their motives are not always clear to themselves, and they may be doing both.

> A group of Girl Scouts decided to have a roller skating party with boys invited. I didn't know how to roller skate very well, and to make matters worse, I didn't like girls. The party turned out to be a free-for-all with the boys chasing the girls around trying to pull their hair. The girls finally fought back which made us very happy. I think the reason why we acted that way was because we didn't know how to act with girls. All the boys agreed that it had been lots of fun, but the girls were quite disappointed. I guess that even at the age of eleven they expected a more romantic attitude on the part of us boys.

In chase-and-touch play, one may be defined by members of the opposite sex as having cooties, which are transferred to others by chasing and touching. Girls, more likely than boys, are the ones designated as having and giving cooties. Girls are the ultimate in untouchables at this age. They may be contaminating through some additional characteristic that stigmatizes them, such as being overweight or poor (Thorne 1985). Thorne (1985:176) found that an occasional boy is also treated as contaminating (for example, a boy who was " 'stinky' " and " 'smelled like pee' "). Boys at the bottom of the boys' hierarchy are sometimes called girls, which also indicates their low status.

Stigmatizing peers, although it plays a role in arriving at status distinctions, is one of the more unpleasant aspects of the teasing that is characteristic among children at this age. Teasing serves many purposes for preadolescents. Besides establishing one child's low status in his or her own gender group as well as across gender lines, it is also used to assert that another child is popular and is accepted in peer interaction. Later on, teasing becomes part of a preromantic type of interaction that reaches a peak among twelve- and thirteen-year-olds, particularly among girls.

Purported romantic liaisons are matters of public notice and widespread rumor and teasing. Sexual and romantic teasing marks preadolescent social hierarchies. It is the most popular children and the pariahs—the lowest status, excluded children—who are most frequently mentioned as targets of liking. Linking someone with a pariah suggests shared contamination and is an especially vicious tease (Thorne and Luria 1985).

Games like chase-and-kiss indicate that there are nascent sexual meanings in cross-gender chasing. The threat of kissing—most often girls threatening to kiss boys—is a ritualized form of provocation. Teachers are more disturbed by it among fifth and sixth graders than they would be if it happened to younger children, perhaps because girls " 'have their development' " (Thorne and Luria 1986:11). In the following case a boy is the chaser and kisser.

> At about age nine, one boy liked both my best friend and me. One day during recess he chased me around the playground. He finally caught me in a parked car in which I was hiding and kissed me fifty times. I felt very good since he had kissed me more than he had my friend, making me sure that he liked me more than her. I enjoyed being kissed by boys since I thought it meant that they loved me and I knew that someday I would love and marry one boy.

As part of their play, even very young children engage in discourse using words that adults think they should not be using or should use with more discretion than they do. When words about body parts and bodily functions are first used, they are used innocently to exchange information or to explain parts of their anatomy. But even preschool children are old enough to discern the provocative value of some "dirty" words to shock or challenge a parent or other adult, or to tease their peers, especially in cross-sex teasing.

Young children like to talk about objects and activities that they sense adults consider dirty or taboo, such as bugs, worms, fleas, pigs, excrement, enemas, and flatulence (Borneman 1983). It is not long before they are capable of learning the even greater provocative power of certain slang words for referring to body parts and bodily sexual functions—words such as cock, cunt, shit, fuck. Gundersen et al. (1981) found a clear tendency for Norwegian nursery school boys to use such sexual words more frequently than did girls but found no gender difference in the selection of words. Borneman (1983) recorded what he regarded as an inordinate number of verses about brother–sister incest and a fair number about parental intercourse in the child culture of Austrian children, all of them appealing to children between ages six and seven.

Dirty words, jokes, rhymes, pictures, and songs play a major part in the communication that goes on among preadolescents. Many of the dirty words are not explicitly sexual. Both boys and girls use them when talking to friends of their own sex, but boys use them much more than girls do; dirty talk is a stable part of their repertoire. Dirty talk is also used in the taunting and teasing that goes on in relations between boys' and girls' groups. Thorne and Luria (1985) found that dirty words were a focus of rules and rule breaking in elementary school. Boys more frequently than girls flaunted dirty words, risking punishment for their use. Fifth- and sixth-grade boys also showed pornography in the form of soft-core magazines like *Playboy* and *Penthouse* and took great care to prevent the material from being confiscated.

Preadolescents spend much of their school day in organized activity under the watchful eyes of principals, teachers, librarians, hall monitors, cafeteria workers, security officers, and others. Given this setting, it is understandable that Thorne and Luria (1986) did not find much activity that could be characterized as directly sexual in nature, for in the presence of teachers girls and boys generally interact in relaxed ways as they do in mixed groups where gender is not made strongly salient. This contrasts markedly to the frenetic activity that often characterizes unsupervised cross-sex interaction on the playground and elsewhere.

Mixed parties are a phenomenon added to the sexual scene in preadolescence. They are fairly common, especially among the middle class. Heterosexual parties are sometimes referred to as group dating; such parties often precede or signal the beginning of paired dating. These parties may be a part of a school activity, they may be planned by organizations of girls, or they may be private parties planned by the youngsters themselves or by their parents.

Many of our parents would arrange for boy–girl parties in their homes, spending their evening upstairs while we were left quite unchaperoned in the basement.

As I recall, the initial party of consequence was a mixed birthday party given in honor of one of the girls. This, more or less, started the run of parties that began to take place nearly every Friday evening during the school year. The kids attending these home parties weren't ever paired off in couples but were invited on an individual basis.

Oftentimes the ratio of boys to girls was uneven—falling either way. The parties throughout the year usually began between 7:30 and 8:00 P.M. and lasted till around 10:00 P.M. when the parents at whose house the party was being held or another "volunteer" would drive the kids home.

For the sake of honors and awards the Chick-a-dee Campfire girls planned parties and hayrides. The boys were not quite as enthusiastic as we hoped they would be, but they came and soon couples developed.

I remember making out invitation lists for parties trying to invite the fellows in whom each of us was interested. Even with all the planning, we never paired off except by more frequent attention given by a favorite during "wink 'um" and "clap-in-clap-out."

In childhood, if there is any pairing off, it is done not because of sexual maturation but primarily because the culture or one's group expects it. A primary group in the form of a gang or clique of a bisexual nature can play an important part in preparing individuals for dating by helping to minimize shyness, fears, frustrations, and anxiety.

There was one girl in particular who was mature physically by the fifth grade and who had ideas of dating before the rest of us did. She was a very strong leader and encouraged the rest of us to date. She seemed to know all the facts of life, and she took advantage of our curiosity at this age and told us all she knew.

Much of first pairing off is hardly distinguishable from girl–boy parties and is usually not formalized, nor is it expected that these relationships will last for long. The relationships are predominantly social rather than sexual. They commonly involve engaging in activities such as riding bikes together, hitting each other playfully, walking home together, smoking together, sitting next to each other at a movie or on the school bus, sharing possessions, attending parties, and even having formal dates with parental support in some cases.

I began dating in the fourth grade. Every Friday night he and I would go to the show and home. His mother chauffeured, and we would hold hands and kiss goodnight.

I don't think our sixth grade boys followed the normal pattern of not liking girls because all of us spent a great deal of time together after school and on weekends. The big romance of the sixth grade was between one of the boys and me. We naturally spent lots of time together at the boy–girl parties and at other times.

During these years (6th–8th grade) we used to sit with a special guy on the bus after basketball games. Going to the games, all of the fellows had to sit in the front of the bus, but going home things would change.

Dating with me began in the seventh grade. It was a companionship relationship and usually consisted of riding our bikes, playing tennis, or going swimming with a bunch of other kids, or the gang would come to my house at night and play group games such as hide-and-seek, starlight-moonlight, etc.

The bravest thing a fellow could do was to find out if the girl you were interested in was going to the show and then appear at the same show and sit next to her. After the show you could walk her home if it was not too far out of your way.

During sixth grade he took me on my first official date—doubling with another couple to the Saturday matinee. He and I developed a great deal of affection for each other, maybe "puppy love" is a better term, and it was quite sad when he moved at the end of the school year.

My mother was quite perturbed when, in the sixth grade, I turned down my first date offer.

My first date was when I was in the sixth grade. There were four couples who went to the Ice Follies by bus all alone. The whole time I was there I can remember being miserable because I wished I was with the girls instead of a boy. After the show we all went over to one of the girls' houses for dinner and dancing. I ran away when my date asked me to dance and then was actually cruel to him the whole evening. I guess I was not ready for a boyfriend just yet, although other girls were beginning.

My first paired dating was in the seventh grade. My friend called for me at home like a perfect gentleman, and gallantly escorted me to the car where his father sat patiently waiting. When the program was over we waited in front of the school for his father to pick us up and take me home.

In communities where it is popular, "going steady" develops as early as the beginning of the preadolescent pairing-off experience (at least it is going steady in the minds of the participants). Symbols of the going-steady status (such as bracelets and rings) are offered and accepted even while the steadies are not in reality dating each other at all, except in their own fantasy world.

After I had been in junior high for a few months I fell in with the going-steady pattern. Before long she asked me to give her a ring or a bracelet of mine which she could wear. After hearing "All the other girls are wearing their boyfriend's rings" many times, I bought a cheap dime-store ring which I gave her. This going-steady period lasted for about five weeks. I never had a date with her or even phoned her during this time. It seems it was all done just to keep up with what other kids were doing.

I began going steady when I was twelve years old and I thought a lot of the boy I was infatuated with. I was sure I had found the secret to happiness and that this was love. My girlfriends also had steady boyfriends and we used to double date. Our dates were not really dates at all but the time we spent together was fun. The boys hardly ever picked us up at our homes. The girls would regularly go to the show Friday nights and Sundays. We would always sit in the same place and the boys would always come and sit with us or behind us. Then after the movie the boys would walk us home. Hardly ever, in fact never, did we take the boys into our homes to talk; we would always stand outside. I do not believe that I ever kissed my boyfriend but we did hold hands in private. I believe that going steady made me feel important and gave me some self-confidence.

Kissing is an activity that many children are familiar with from early childhood. They have kissed and been kissed by their parents, their siblings, relatives, and sometimes their playmates. There is provocative kissing in chase-and-kiss, sometimes an unserious play kiss confined to a smack on the cheek or a brief brushing of the lips (Rainwater 1970) as well as more serious goal-directed kissing. Kissing is frequently marked by excitement, erotic overtones, confusion, embarrassment, guilt, disgust, or some combination of these.

A series of make-out parties which I enjoyed began in the fourth grade. Liking to kiss people came naturally from my affectionate surroundings, and I made good use of it.

Sixth grade finally rolled around and I was in the "in group." We all had to have a boyfriend, so I got one. My girlfriends began to have boy–girl parties on weekend nights. I just hated going to them. My boyfriend always wanted to kiss. I pretended like I liked it, but I really wanted to throw up all over him. It just grossed me out. The guilt feelings ran really high. I was afraid my parents would find out, and I lived in fear.

Everyone at mixed-couple parties sat on the couch with the lights out and kissed. I, a 7th grade girl, was so embarrassed and confused at such activity that I left the party early, went home and cried. I hated that boy from then on and refused to go anyplace with him.

In whatever way it first occurred, she and I (9–10 years old) began to try out simple methods of love-making, such as kissing and embracing. Although I could not ascertain it clearly at the time, there seemed to be a distinctly warm and comfortable feeling in what we were doing. This probably marked my first real sexual attraction toward the opposite sex.

Parties involving dancing, and sometimes slow dancing with close body contact, occur during preadolescence in homes and in the school. Like kissing, dancing can bring its moments of ecstasy and moments of unpleasantness.

When I entered junior high school there weren't many fellows who were on the dance floor at school dances. They were all in a group in the corner and that is where I ended up too. We told jokes, tested our strength on the bars that stood along the walls, and teased any fellow who dared to ask a girl to dance.

I remember one of the chaperones. Whenever she found a couple dancing a little closer than she thought was proper, she would shove the ruler between the couple and say, "Six inches apart, children."

The ability to dance caused a new type of party to evolve. The girls planned these parties, which always centered around the slow dance. These parties usually started slow and inhibited, the boys grouping on one side of the room and the girls on the other. As the party progressed, however, the boys, due to group support, gathered up enough courage to ask a girl to dance. The dancing was of the "cheek-to-cheek" kind and if the girl had no reservations about whom she was dancing with, the couple usually stuck together throughout the entire evening.

At our parties there was a small amount of dancing and a large amount of games. This consisted of embarrassing things for me. They were winkum, passing life savers with tooth-picks, etc.

I would have preferred other games to dancing. For me this came too early and pushed me faster than I wanted to grow up; however, I was caught up in the false social whirl of this group and began to think as they did.

Activities of a group or paired nature during preadolescence sometimes change from games or dancing into more intimate caressing and fondling experiences, referred to by the ambiguous euphemism "making out."

We'd start out by playing games like "spin the bottle." Later everyone would pair off. After we had coupled up for the evening, we usually had contests, such as what couple could hold a kiss the longest, etc.

The lights were shut off or the parents would leave and the "necking" aspect of the party would begin. The silence of the party would be broken intermittently by someone "cracking a joke," changing a record or getting up to dance.

During fifth and sixth grade home parties, she and I always managed to get together. More often than not we crept away to a quiet corner of the cellar and began doing "our things." Kissing and tight embraces proved to be the extent of our actions, but the opportunity for such behavior occurred quite frequently.

I was in the seventh grade. There were only couples there. We ate and danced for a while and then everyone sat on the couch with the lights out and kissed.

The slow songs and dim lights seemed like heaven, with a stiff penis being the first pleasurable sign. Sometimes the girl and myself would hold each other tighter as the songs progressed and many times, about halfway through a song, we would start to touch bottoms and really hold each other tight—oh, I hoped the songs would never end. This sometimes led to making out after a few songs or just holding hands, but whatever it was it was really "neat."

Boy–girl mutual genital fondling is not a universal experience of preadolescent couples in the United States, but it is not unknown either. Ramsey (1943) reported that sexual experiences, when they did occur for boys, most frequently involved manual manipulation associated with direct observation of each other's bodies. Exhibitionistic sex play was the next most frequent type of behavior.

We both had reached the ripe old age of twelve. Sexual experimentation was not new to me nor to him. That evening after dark we met secretly at a secluded spot. We kissed for a while and both of us became increasingly excited. This led, in turn, to the unfastening of our clothes and the placement of his hand on my breast. Gradually his hand crept downwards, beneath my pants until he was gently stroking my mon veneris and clitoris. He wanted to "finger" me but I resisted firmly as a girl had to draw the line somewhere! Now he posed a rather surprising question. He wanted "me" to touch "him." He exposed his erect penis and pulled my hand toward it. At the thought of touching it I trembled, but managed to do so. I think I was the first girl in seventh grade to actually "feel out" a boy as this was previously unheard of. We continued to mutually masturbate for a while and then I decided that it was time for me to go home. The significance of this encounter lies in the fact that for the first time one of my childhood experiences had suddenly become really sexual, and the action was tinged with my first feelings of guilt. I suffered a great deal following this incident for fear of losing my reputation.

Whether or not children engage in simulated or actual sexual intercourse depends on the way they have been brought up and how knowledgeable they are. In the following two cases of simulated intercourse, the boy is more naive than the girl.

My girlfriend and I—I 5 and she 6—used to ride our bikes together, play house, etc. One day, while playing indoors, she expressed a desire to take our pants off. This seemed a mere violation of the nudity taboo rather than anything related to sex, as I had no knowledge of such things. We undressed, she laid on her back on the bed with her legs spread apart. I got an erection, which pleased her. She told me to roll over on top of her. This seemed like a strange thing to do, but I decided to comply. Just then my mother entered the room.

She asked me if I wanted to see her genitals. I didn't know what she meant, but it sounded mysterious and I was interested. We went to our secret hiding place and she told me what to do. To kiss her genitals and to put myself on her and to push and get back. I didn't get very much out of it.

Some societies are considerably more permissive than U.S. society, encouraging—or at least not discouraging—child sexual behavior (Ford and Beach 1951). In communities where parents speak openly about sex and place no taboos on physical contact, exploration of each other's bodies and actual intercourse takes place between children as young as five or six years of age. Sexual life begins in earnest among Trobriand Island children at six to eight years for girls and ten to twelve years for boys. Sex play includes masturbation, oral stimulation of the genitals of the same and opposite sex, and heterosexual copulation. At any time a couple may retire to the bush, the bachelors' hut, an isolated yam house, or any convenient place and there engage in prolonged sexual play. Among the Ila-speaking peoples of Africa, this is regarded as a time of preparation for adult life and mature sexual functioning. It is reported that there are no virgins among these people after the age of ten. The Lapcha of India believe that girls will not mature without the benefit of sexual intercourse. Early sex play for boys and girls in that society characteristically involves many forms of mutual masturbation and usually ends in attempted copulation. By the time they are eleven or twelve years old, most girls regularly engage in sexual intercourse.

Johnston and Deisher (1973) found that children in a permissive American commune related to sex as something interesting and enjoyable but not as of central importance to their play activity. Such permissiveness is not characteristic of many American communities, yet Ramsey (1943) found that in his sample of primarily middle and upper-middle socioeconomic level Midwestern urban boys, 6 percent had had heterosexual intercourse by age six, 11 percent by age seven, and 16 percent by age eight. We do not have comparable data for girls or boys from more recent periods. At every age in childhood, boys tend to engage in more sexual activity than do girls.

First experiments with copulation are not unusual for American children between the ages of ten and fourteen. By twelve years of age, approximately one boy in every four or five has at least attempted to copulate with a female, and more than 10 percent of preadolescent boys experience their first ejaculation in connection with heterosexual intercourse, according to Kinsey et al. (1948). Preadolescent attempts to have genital union occurred in nearly 22 percent of all male histories, which is over half (55%) of the histories of boys who had engaged in preadolescent heterosexual play. Ramsey (1943) reported that about one third of his sample of middle-class boys had attempted sexual intercourse. The incidence of heterosexual involvement varies with the socioeducational level, being least frequent for preadolescents who eventually go to college (Kinsey et al. 1948). The lower-level boys had considerable information and assistance in these matters from older boys or from adult males, and in many cases their first heterosexual contacts were with older girls who had already had experience.

For these boys coitus may have occurred with some frequency and with a variety of partners.

Kinsey et al. (1948) found considerable evidence that preadolescents recognized oral contacts as taboo; nevertheless, American preadolescents occasionally practice oral sex play. Mouth–genital contact occurs in about 2 percent of cases of girls and 9 percent of cases of boys who have had heterosexual play experience.

> After stripping girls, beginning in the second and third grade, my curiosity led me to touch, smell, and eventually to taste that hole.

In sum, even in a society such as ours that goes to great pains to restrict sexual activity among children, children go through stages of heterosexual development. In some communities and socioeconomic groups, these stages begin in preadolescence or earlier. The stages also take longer or shorter to complete depending on sexual and social maturity, the permissiveness of superiors, and the support of peers. In preadolescence, if not before, youngsters form attachments or crushes on persons outside the family. The love feeling is expressed to the other person in a form that depends on the youngster's age, sexual and social maturity, permissiveness of superiors, and the support of peers. It may appear in the form of rough-house love play (hitting a boy, pulling girls' hair), writing notes, inviting to a party, or simply walking someone home. If the other person responds to this attention, the two may enter into the first of what often turns out to be a long series of close relationships with peers of the opposite sex. Some are informal and relaxed; others are formal and intense. Some involve sexual experiment; others do not. Often a sexual experience is part of a specific school setting or occasion such as an athletic event, a band or play rehearsal, a visit to relatives (cousins are favorite objects of attention), or a party with peers. There is little doubt that these encounters with their varying degrees of emotional involvement are important at the time that they occur and influence later attitudes toward love, sex, and the opposite sex. They also provide a set of learning experiences, including such obvious things as learning how to kiss, how to dance, how to talk to a person of the opposite sex, and how to fondle and caress. The process of learning these skills is often exciting and dramatic but also anxious and embarrassing. A college student, on reading about stages of heterosexual experience in preadolescence, wrote the following:

> As I recall, this was a period of great experimentation, exposure, and discussion of sex. Elaborate games which we thought disguised our

motives quite well were created in order that we might expose ourselves in what seemed to be a permissible manner. The fourth grade was characterized by serious boy–girl relationships in which "making out" was a vital component. In the fifth and sixth grade the boys my age were getting their thrills, much to the horror of us girls, by taking pictures of each other experiencing an erection. The longer I spend recalling attitudes, conversations, and actions of the six to twelve age group, the more convinced I am that this certainly was no latency period.

The trend toward more active sexual lives among adolescents is also reflected in the lives of some preadolescents. Girls who are as young as twelve show up at health clinics, schools, and parenting programs. It is not that there are so many pregnancies under age thirteen, but the number receives a great deal of media attention and publicity. Preadolescent pregnancies do present special problems for community agencies. There were only four girls known to Hennepin County's (Minnesota) family service division in 1992, but that number does represent an increase (Hopfensperger 1993). It was unusual for a twelve-year-old girl to have a steady boyfriend and to engage in an active sexual life in the 1970s. It is not just lack of information on birth control and sex education that is at the heart of the problem. Many of the girls come from troubled family relationships, and they lack the acceptance and feeling of self-esteem necessary to say no to sexual intercourse. Without self-esteem it is very difficult to reverse the trend of male dependency and early birth of children that is characteristic of girls this age.

NOTE

1. There is no single criterion by which the onset of adolescence is recognized. For males, Kinsey et al. (1948) regarded the date of first ejaculation as signaling the onset. In 85 percent of Kinsey's male histories, first ejaculation occurred in the same year as first appearance of pubic hair, onset of rapid growth in height, and/or certain other developments. If there had been no test of ejaculation but these other changes had occurred, they were used as determining the onset of adolescence. In girls, the onset of adolescence was regarded as the period in which there is an increased rate of physical growth and the final development of reproductive function (Kinsey et al. 1953).

The age of onset of adolescence is often construed legally as fourteen years in boys and twelve years in girls, recognizing the later onset of adolescence in boys.

REFERENCES

Bell, S. "A Preliminary Study of the Emotion of Love between the Sexes." *American Journal of Psychology* XIII(1902):325–54.

Borneman, E. "Progress in Empirical Research on Children's Sexuality." *SIECUS Report* 12(1983):1–6.

Ford, C. S. and F. A. Beach. *Patterns of Sexual Behavior*. New York: Harper, 1951.

Gundersen, B. H., P. S. Melås, and J. E. Skår. "Sexual Behavior of Preschool Children: Teachers' Observations." In *Children and Sex: New Findings, New Perspectives*, edited by L. L. Constantine and F. M. Martinson, 45–61. Boston: Little, Brown, 1981.

Hopfensperger, Jean. "Looking for Someone to Love: Ranks of Under-15 Mothers Growing." *Star Tribune* (July 6, 1993):1A, 9A.

Johnston, C. and R. W. Deisher. "Contemporary Communal Child Rearing: A First Analysis." *Pediatrics* 52(1973):319–26.

Kinsey, A. C., W. B. Pomeroy, and C. E. Martin. *Sexual Behavior in the Human Male*. Philadelphia: W. B. Saunders, 1948.

Kinsey, A. C., W. B. Pomeroy, C. E. Martin, and P. H. Gebhard. *Sexual Behavior in the Human Female*. Philadelphia: W. B. Saunders, 1953.

Rainwater, L. *Behind Ghetto Walls: Black Families in a Federal Slum*. Chicago: Aldine, 1970.

Ramsey, G. V. "The Sexual Development of Boys." *American Journal of Psychology* 56(1943):217–33.

Spiro, M. E. *Children of the Kevutza*. Cambridge, Mass.: Harvard University, 1958.

Thorne, B. "Girls and Boys Together . . . But Mostly Apart: Gender Arrangements in Elementary Schools." In *Relationships and Development*, edited by W. W. Hartup and Z. Rubin, 161–84. Hillsdale, N.J.: Lawrence Erlbaum Associates, 1985.

Thorne, B. and Z. Luria. "Sexuality and Gender in Children's Daily Worlds." *Social Problems* 33(1986):176–80.

4

Same-Sex Sex Play

Young children play with either boys or girls, and they are not discriminating in their choice of play activity. But they soon learn that their parents have ideas about what activities they should engage in and with whom they should engage in them. Since older children spend much of their play time in segregated boys' and girls' worlds, it is understandable that much of their sexual curiosity, sex talk, and sexual experimentation is played out in association with same-sex peers.

Same-sex sex play is not generally approved of in U.S. society, but this is not universally true in human societies. Ford and Beach (1957) found that the majority (64%) of the seventy-six societies (other than U.S. society) on which data are available consider same-sex sexual activity as normal and socially acceptable at least for certain members of the community or for certain periods of life. For the Keraki of New Guinea, for instance, a man was regarded as abnormal if he abstained from such relations prior to marriage, and the Kiwai had the custom of practicing sodomy in connection with initiation to make a young man strong. Among the North American Crow a few men, called *bate*, adopted women's dress and mannerisms and lived alone. One of their activities was the oral stimulation of boys' genitals; adolescent boys and occasionally older men visited the *bate* as well.

Ford and Beach's cross-cultural comparisons led them to three generalizations concerning same-sex sexual activity. First, there is a wide divergence of social attitudes toward it. Second, no matter how it is treated in any particular society, the behavior will likely occur among some persons. Third, males seem more likely to engage in same-sex sexual activity than do females. All three conclusions are applicable to the situation in the United States. Child guidance professionals who give advice to parents on how to react to child sexual experiences recognize that peer sex play does occur, but their acceptance of it is not without reservation (Martinson 1992).

In this chapter, we look at children's same-sex sexual activity for the same reason that we look at all child sexual activity, mainly to understand more about the life of children, not to determine the predictive power of same-sex activity. Sexual behavior of children, either same- or other-sex, has been found to have little or no predictive power.

Same-sex sexual play in childhood in the United States is usually episodic in occurrence, often being confined to one, two, or a few experiences and only during a short period of life. This is especially true for females. In Kinsey et al.'s study of females (1953), which included a review of earlier studies, females reporting same-sex contact varied from 4 percent in one study to as high as 26 percent in several studies. Only a fraction of 1 percent of females recalled sex play with girls as having occurred as early as three years of age. Six percent recalled such play by age five, 15 percent by age seven, 25 percent by age nine, and 33 percent by the onset of adolescence. Most of the same-sex play had been confined, as had girl–boy sex play, to a single year and one or two experiences for the majority of girls with same-sex experience. About half of older males in the Kinsey et al. study of males (1948) and 60 percent of boys who were preadolescents at the time they contributed their histories recalled same-sex activity. Twelve percent reported that such behavior occurred at five years of age and 17 percent at age ten.

In the Ramsey study (1943), approximately half of the boys who had been involved in preadolescent same-sex play had confined their relationship to one other boy. The remaining boys with such experience reported from two to ten partners. The partners were, except in rare instances, boys of approximately the same age. The frequency of same-sex play ranged from a single experience to a maximum of over 400 experiences.

Exposing, exploring, and manual manipulation are the most common same-sex activities among children. For both sexes, genital exhibitionism is by far the most common, with approximately 99 percent of females and 99.8 percent of males with same-sex experience reporting it (Kinsey et al. 1948, 1953). Exhibition appears mostly among the youngest children. Much of it is incidental, casual, and fruitless as far as erotic arousal is concerned (Kinsey et al. 1948), as in the following three cases.

> My friend and I were behind the furnace in the basement. He dropped his trousers, bent over, and spread his cheeks for me to get a good look. I exclaimed. Then I did the same for him and he exclaimed.

At the age of six or seven my friend and I had a great curiosity for exploring the anus. It almost seemed more like scientific research.

Normal play took up about 90 percent of the play of my constant play mate and me, but we also had an intense fascination with each other's bodies and their functions. Elimination was a constant source of interest and we would take turns watching each other urinate and defecate. There was no sexual fascination that I remember, simply a tremendous curiosity.

With boys, same-sex activity often has a tinge of competitiveness attached to it; for example, a mother reports that she saw two boys giggling excitedly while having a contest to see which one could "wee wee" the farthest (Sears, Maccoby, and Levine 1957). Such activity is likely both low in erotic intent and satisfaction. At older ages the competitiveness sometimes involves competition around physical maturity.

I was invited to an all-boy slumber party. We were all in the seventh grade. Someone suggested that we play strip poker. A couple of fellows, including myself, protested but finally the majority ruled. (I was embarrassed because of my obvious lack of any signs of physical maturity.) I was one of the losers. About two of us ended up stark naked, while the others were in various stages of undress. No sex play resulted at this juncture, except for the obvious visual effect. We all hurriedly got dressed when we heard the host's mother coming.

Exhibition often leads into manipulation of the genitals. In the Kinsey sample of boys (1948), 67 percent of all those with same-sex experience had engaged in such manipulation. Only a slightly smaller percentage of girls (62%) had engaged in manual manipulation of the genitals.

She dared me to touch her breasts. I was very afraid and repulsed by the idea, but I did it because I didn't want her to see I was afraid. When she touched my breasts, I really enjoyed it. I felt a tingling all over my body that I had never felt before.

During the sixth grade, whenever we stayed overnight we slept in the same bed. We began experimenting and fondling each other's breasts. We tested for size and who could feel the other out the best. We never thought we were "queer"—we were trying to find out what it would be like if a guy did this to us.

For some reason we found that we enjoyed our friendship better than those we had with members of the opposite sex. From the time we met, up until about the time of fifth grade, she and I played a game which we enjoyed very much. We would see older couples holding hands, lying on the beach, swimming, picnicking, etc., and then we would proceed to imitate their actions with each other. She would always play the boy's role and I the girl's. There was nothing physical about our actions other than a caress here or there. This game played a significant part in our friendship, and seemed to provide us with security.

We played these pretending games for hours at a time over approximately two years, but only during the winter months. Our games all amounted to the same basic idea: playing the roles of boyfriend and girlfriend, taking turns being the "boy." It was much more fun to be the girl, to be submissive and have to struggle and protest a bit. (We were definitely not concerned with the Women's Liberation Movement.) Our favorite situation was pretending to be teenagers when one of our homes had been vacated by the parents. I am quite sure that the only cause of my being "turned-on" by sexual contact was my fascination that my partner was a "boy."

Much of manual manipulation among boys involves masturbating in each other's presence or mutually masturbating each other.

When I was 10, my friend and I were playing in a house under construction. He was one floor above me; we could see each other through a knothole. I told him to stick his "cock" through the hole. I pulled a ladder over below him. After touching his "cock" a couple of times, I told him we should switch positions. He decided to grab my organ and pull, to which I objected. We switched positions again, and he urinated on my hand after a while. This ended the adventure.

We often engaged in mutual exploration of genitals and anus. We would fully undress and take turns exploring. We both had erections and would masturbate, although we didn't know what it was. He was circumcised and I was not so this caused some interest. During these times neither of us engaged in any talking.

When I was about 12, I had a completely different experience. Some of us boys got together one night and had a "circle jerk"; we stood around in a circle each holding onto the boy's penis in back of us.

Several of us were sleeping over. I laid down next to one of my friends, and we talked for a long time. I remember scratching his back and then he asked me if I would itch his "cock." I guess it was more curiosity than anything that led me to comply. I had heard the word masturbate before, but I had no idea what it meant. Anyway, I was stimulating him and he all of a sudden insisted that I stop. He then suggested that he return the favor. He began to stimulate me, and the sensation was so great at orgasm I made him stop for second. Then I asked him to start again and the sensation came back and I made him stop again. I was too young to ejaculate anything, but it sure felt good. We repeated the cycle at least ten times before we quit.

Sex play that includes oral-genital manipulation occurs more commonly among boys than among girls; in the Kinsey et al. studies (1948, 1953), 3 percent of females and 16 percent of males who had some same-sex experience remembered it occurring.

My best friend and I engaged in sex play between five and ten times during fifth through seventh grade. We would examine each other's genitals and occasionally engage in oral-genital contact. Playing doctor usually ended up by agreeing to "suck your dink if you suck mine."

Masturbating together went on until one day he told me what a "blow job" was and wanted me to give him one. I made a feeble attempt at it but I thought it tasted awful.

At five years of age we had a club. One of the other boys wanted to do more experimenting than just exposing ourselves and each watching the opposite sex urinate. His and my experimenting consisted of mutual fondling of penises and also fellating each other.

Inserting something into the anus or urethra of a boy or into the vagina of a girl is another same-sex experience not uncommon in childhood. According to Kinsey et al. (1953), 18 percent of girls remembered experiences where objects, at least fingers, were inserted in vaginas, compared to only 3 percent remembering such insertions when they played with boys. Seventeen percent of boys recalled play with other boys in which there were insertions in the anus (Kinsey et al. 1948). When anal intercourse was attempted, penetration usually failed, resulting primarily in femoral contact. Six percent of the boys reported urethral insertions.

I encountered a sexual experience at kindergarten age that was confusing. Some afternoons we would meet and lock ourselves in a bedroom and take our pants off. We took turns lying on the bed and put pennies, marbles, etc. between our labia. The other two liked to pretend they were boys and used a pencil for a penis. As the ritual became old hat, it passed out of existence. I enjoyed the sexual manipulation, for it was stimulating. Yet, I never wanted to pretend that I had a penis.

On the whole, Kinsey et al. (1948) found more same-sex play in the histories of boys; it occurred more frequently among them; and it became more specific in type of activity than did sex play for girls. This higher incidence depended in part on the greater accessibility of boys as companions in play among boys who belonged to boy's organizations.

Probably the most misleading sex education I received was in the Boy Scout organization. If Baden Powell knew what perverted acts and latent homosexual tendencies came about on camping trips, he would probably roll over in his grave.

The Boy Scout organization allowed many of my more inclined peers the opportunity for sex play with each other.

Fewer parents set limits on physical contact between same-sex playmates than they do on children with their opposite-sex friends. Berges et al. (1983) found that when parents did set limits on same-sex touching, they did not usually mention concern about homosexuality as a reason; nevertheless it seemed to be implicitly present in their thoughts. A few parents said they did not make any distinctions on the basis of sex in setting standards for their children's touching behavior with their friends; occasionally, the age of the children involved was mentioned as more important than their sex.

The Project on Human Sexual Development (Roberts, Kline, and Gagnon 1978) sponsored a two-year interview study in Cleveland, Ohio, of parents' attitudes and behavior regarding the sexual learning of their children. Over 1,400 mothers and fathers from dual- and single-parent families were interviewed. Each parent interviewed was the mother or father of a child between the ages of three and eleven. Parents seemed to accept homosexuality as a reality, but for most it was a disturbing reality and one they hoped would not reach their families. Fathers were more likely than mothers to caution their sons verbally not to act like sissies and their daughters not to act like tomboys. They generally began to talk with their sons about acting like a boy or a little man and not like a sissy at about the time they entered school, while there appeared to be a longer grace period for girls, with parents not evidencing concern about their daughters' boyish behavior until right before puberty. Too much touching, especially among boys, appeared to cause discomfort for a number of parents. From indications in many families, fear of homosexuality often prevented open and shared affection between fathers and sons and inhibited children's learning about their bodies. Most boys were discouraged from kissing, hugging, being gentle, or even asking for comfort or help. A number of parents wanted to find ways to encourage their sons to be emotionally expressive, but the responses, particularly of fathers, indicated that they had difficulty in modeling the kinds of behaviors they would like their children to learn. Parents indicated a desire to have assistance in dealing with the topic of homosexuality. They were concerned about what to tell their children about it; many were uncertain about the causes of homosexuality and were fearful of it. Consequently, they tended to monitor their own behavior and the behavior of their child lest "something happen" and the child indicate a homosexual preference.

REFERENCES

Ford, C. S. and F. A. Beach. *Patterns of Sexual Behavior*. New York: Harper, 1951.

Kinsey, A. C., W. B. Pomeroy, and C. E. Martin. *Sexual Behavior in the Human Male*. Philadelphia: W. B. Saunders, 1948.

Kinsey, A. C., W. B. Pomeroy, C. E. Martin, and P. H. Gebhard. *Sexual Behavior in the Human Female*. Philadelphia: W. B. Saunders, 1953.

Ramsey, G. V. "The Sexual Development of Boys." *American Journal of Psychology* 56(1943):217–33.

Roberts, E. J., D. Kline, and J. Gagnon. *Family Life and Sexual Learning, A Study of the Rule of Parents in the Sexual Learning of Children*. Cambridge, Mass.: Population Education Inc., 1978.

Sears, R. R., E. E. Maccoby, and H. Levine. *Patterns of Child Rearing*. Evanston, Ill.: Row, Peterson, 1957.

5

Dreams, Fantasies, and Myths

One way to ascertain the extent of sexual knowledge and sexual experience of children is to look at content in their fantasy world as revealed in their dreams, stories, and myths. Fantasy activity *per se* is universal in human life, representing the ongoing baseline mental activity of humans. Attending to this internal mental activity is behavior learned early in childhood (Rosenfeld et al. 1982). Dreams occur during sleep, while fantasies occur during waking hours; they are similar enough that fantasies are also called daydreams. It is assumed that sometime in the first year of life, before they begin to speak, children begin to fantasize (Gardner 1969). In studies of child play it has been found that young children are very comfortable with fantasy and are able to move quickly and easily from reality to fantasy and back again (Martinson 1992). Children's styles of fantasy are remarkably similar to those of adults, except that fanciful daydreaming appears mostly unique to children (Rosenfeld et al. 1982).

> Fantasy was very often practiced, at any time of mental inactivity. When my actual sexual knowledge was lowest, sadistic ideas and perversions were often fantasized, replaced in time by a more accurate and acceptable fantasy content. As far as fantasy is concerned, the ideas I devised were usually far worse without knowledge than my fantasy developed through knowledge towards actions that married couples usually practice. I would say that before the age of 13, fantasy was either very innocent of erotic concepts, or very sadistic and violent through ignorance.

During or subsequent to genital self-stimulation in the second year of life, both girls and boys frequently make affectional gestures toward their mothers and touch their mothers' bodies. But such open affection begins to disappear after a few weeks and is replaced by an "inward gaze and a self-absorbed look" that soon begins to occur, indicating that a fantasy feeling-state now becomes a regular part of genital stimulation (Roiphe and Galenson 1981:252).

One might expect that the fantasy feeling-state accompanying genital play would show up in the stories young children tell, but it does not appear to do so, not for American children, for American children learn very early that they must not talk about sex, at least not in the presence of adults. That is one reason why the subject of sex does not commonly appear in their stories. An inability or unwillingness to use words referring to sex was one of the most striking findings of Conn's play interview study of 200 children four to fourteen years of age (Conn and Kanner 1947; see also Kanner 1939).

In his play interviews, Conn found that sexual fantasies accompanying masturbation—imagining the sight or touch of genitals, buttocks, or breasts, and thoughts of coitus—were reported by a very small number of boys below nine years and by no girls of any age. For instance, in play interviews, the children even as young as four years of age spoke hesitatingly and without embarrassment of the boy's "thing" and the girl's "thing," but other distinctions had something secret or hidden about them. It was not so much that they did not know names for the genitals; in fact, Conn found no less than sixty-one different names for genitals among the 200 children. But the children regarded these names as bad, nasty, or dirty and hence not to be uttered in the presence of adults. Children with such inhibitions can hardly be expected to report stories they make up or dreams they have had about sex and sexual activity. Another reason for the lack of stories about sex is limited information and lack of sexual experience. With more information and/or experience, children's fantasy life changes. This is evident in some of the cases reported later in this chapter.

There have been two major studies of the stories told by young children (Ames 1966; Pitcher and Prelinger 1963). Ames found that in children two to four years of age, the predominant theme at every age for both boys and girls was violence. Of fifteen two-year-old boys (mean age 2.5), 60 percent of the stories dealt with violence, and for fifteen girls the figure was 68 percent. Other themes in the stories to two-year-olds were: food and eating (boys 14%, girls 27%); sleep (boys 77%, girls 28%); good and bad (boys 0%, girls 21%); possible sibling rivalry (boys 21%, girls 7%); possible castration (boys 14%, girls 0%); and reproduction (boys 0%, girls 7%). None of the group of thirty two-year-olds described stories overtly concerned with anal activity.

Of Pitcher and Prelinger's 137 two- to five-year-olds, eight main themes were found: aggression, death, hurt or misfortune, morality, nutrition, dress, sociability, and crying. Aggression appeared most often—124 times in 360 stories; hurt and misfortune was the next most frequent theme, appearing eighty-nine times. For boys, aggression tended to be much more violent than for girls. Even at two and three years of age, the boys' calamities involved much violence. Boys reported to Ramsey (1943) on dream content in which they found themselves with erections on awakening. The dream content contained nonerotic but potentially violent stimuli—fighting, accidents, wild animals, falling from high places, giants, or being chased or frightened.

Among Pitcher and Prelinger's two-year-olds, the theme was largely concerned with violence of body intactness—some part of the body was broken or severed. The interest in this theme, especially among boys, would appear to be consistent with fears of castration. This theme was almost absent in the stories of three-year-old boys, however. Gardner (1969), based on clinical experience, does not believe that castration anxiety is a significant concern for the normal boy, nor is penis envy a preoccupation in the well-adjusted girl. Rather, the healthy child accepts his or her sex and has pride both in the sexual and nonsexual aspects of the self.

For Ames (1966), the number of stories featuring some kind of violence ranged from a low of 63 percent for boys at two years to a high of 88 percent of boys at three and a half years. The next most common theme was aggression. Ames also found boys to be much more violent in their expression than were girls. In general, Ames found spanking to be strong in the early age as well. Ames concluded, "If it should be that they absorb the violence from the culture, then such absorption must be considered a rather universal phenomenon expressing itself as early as two years of age" (Ames 1966:390).

The following case is an interesting self-analysis of the fantasizing of aggression with some sexual feeling mixed in.

> I can only vaguely remember an episode which took place when I was no more than three or four years old. This is the first sexual experience I can recall having. In one of my children's fairy tale books was a picture which attracted my attention. I would spend long periods of time studying it intently. I cannot remember much about the picture other than that it was of a young child—I don't recall the sex. The child was wearing sleepers like the ones I had, and was sitting with its own fairy tale book in its lap. The child was yawning and rubbing its fist in its eye, signifying, I suppose, that it was sleepy. Looking at that picture I can remember a strange and different feeling came over me,

something that was vague, something that I hadn't remembered experiencing before. I would identify it now as a feeling of aggression and at the same time a sexual feeling. I can vaguely recall a strange sensation emanating from my loins. I felt like I wanted to hit that child and yell at it; why, I don't know. That is all I can remember from the situation; I don't know if I manipulated or touched my genitals in that circumstance or if I had an erection.

But what of themes that relate to the sensory and sexual experiences of life—intimacy, kindness, eroticism? Ames (1966) found that though kind and friendly stories were not very common at any age from two to five years, they sometimes occurred at two and three years of age. Pitcher and Prelinger (1963) found that girls sometimes referred to love, courtship, and marriage. The girls were more likely than the boys to express emotion and affect around a parental figure, particularly a mother. The boys displayed an extraordinary lack of interaction with either mother or father. Pitcher and Prelinger found that it was rare that the phenomenon of excitement and of aggression between a man and a woman took place in the stories. They attributed this in part to the taboo on sexual knowledge for children in the United States and the fact that adults keep most aspects of their own sex life secret. The younger infants appeared at times to make transparent references to the issue of pregnancy in their stories, but the connection of the various details tended commonly to be illogical or poorly motivated. Gardner (1969) agreed with Ames and Pitcher and Prelinger that the conscious fantasy life of the normal child at this age contains little overt sexual material. But Gardner found that from about age eight and onward, sexual fantasies might take any form known to adults. It may be a phase-specific theme that the culture does not allow or encourage to be more specific and accurate among younger children. But Pitcher and Prelinger (1963) did not rule out the possibility that manifestations of unconscious (or more or less conscious) preoccupation with sexuality are prevalent in many of the stories of young children. In the following case a preadolescent girl attributes part of her sexual awakening to sex dream experience.

Wild and confused dreams made me feel funny—just as if I had to urinate. The dreams included boys and girls kissing, and the funny feeling I got was both distressing and exciting. I had no idea as to what the dreams meant, but I definitely realized that they pertained to sex.

In neither of the two studies nor in Gardner's clinical observations do the fantasies of children reflect any sensual-sexual experience in the family. It will be recalled, however, that Borneman (1983), in gathering information about the content of forbidden riddles, songs, verses, and games in Austria, reported what he regarded as an inordinate number of verses about brother–sister incest and a fair number about parental intercourse—all of them in stories appealing to children between ages six and seven. This may reflect cultural differences in the exposure of children to sexual knowledge and sexual experience, but it more likely reflects a difference in methods of soliciting information from children.

Wermer and Levin (1967) distinguished between two kinds of erotic fantasies, erotic fantasies in general and masturbation fantasies in particular; they did so in the following way. Erotic fantasies consist of all types of fantasies of a sexual nature, including those that could become reality if the person being fantasized about were available as a participant with the one who is fantasizing. Masturbation fantasies, on the other hand, are sometimes of a kind that could not be fulfilled in any reality relationship with another person. In addition, the aim of masturbation fantasy is self-gratification, and the person masturbating may have little or no desire to translate his or her masturbation fantasy into action. In the masturbation history of a healthy person, masturbation fantasies tend to undergo a variety of changes as the person passes through different phases of psychosexual development. First masturbation for young, innocent children is apt to be accompanied by fantasy content that, as described by one young man, is "either very innocent of erotic concepts or very sadistic and violent through ignorance." As one person stated,

> The fantasy in connecting with masturbation, running from highly sadistic to just an ordinary sexual intercourse relationship, seemed to parallel the development of my sexual interest.

The following are some examples of young children's perverse and violent sex dreams and fantasies.

> I began to masturbate after the third grade, when I was between the ages of nine and ten. (I could have begun earlier; my memory is hazy about how old I was.) I would come home from school in the afternoon to an empty house. I would grab a snack and sit in front of the television, and I would masturbate. Even from the start I always masturbated to orgasm and often had multiple orgasms (two or three). I usually had a fantasy about slave girls being stripped naked and humiliated and mistreated by a jeering crowd or by one man.

I tended to have masochistic fantasies during masturbation. I would imagine that I was being tortured and twist or stretch my penis, so there was a degree of pain as well as pleasure. Sometimes I would also push things up my rectum, such as the end of a toothbrush, that would also add to my "torture" fantasy.

My first masturbation fantasies involved me (a girl) being held captive by a gang of boys, having to perform rituals including intercourse with them all, and showing my body to the group.

Besides masturbation as part of my childhood experience, I had a dream that I dreamt several times. It was about my elementary school teachers being captured, stripped and tied up in the cafeteria. I was an onlooker and saw a man torture the teachers. He would force couples to have sexual intercourse, cut off breasts from the ladies and penises from the men. I couldn't figure out any reason to have this type of dream. I always liked my teachers, nude people were nothing new to me, and I didn't have any sex hang-ups.

The following are examples of what would be regarded as more normal sexual fantasies.

The thing that really got me on this track is the fact that my father had a subscription to *Playboy*. I was able to sneak a magazine into my room and while looking at it I would masturbate and fantasize that I was in the picture with the girl myself. I would think I was having intercourse with her and the procedure worked quite well to excite me. I was sort of having a love affair with the picture instead of the real thing. I masturbated quite often; most of the time with a *Playboy* in my hand.

I remember the first time I used pictures to accompany my masturbation fantasies. While looking at *Life* magazine I came across a color spread of Renaissance portraits and scenes showing partially naked women. These pictures gave me an erection so I used them in my fantasies while masturbating. From then on I would use pictures frequently, but I only used the same picture several times. After that their novelty would wear off. Later, quite by accident, I found some pornographic magazines. I brought them home and hid them and would haul them out when I was alone. During this time (fourth and fifth grade), I probably masturbated three or four times a week on the average, but possibly more.

My only sexual outlet was fantasizing while masturbating. I was turned on by girls and sex but was so shy and tied to home by mother that I couldn't do much. I never went to dances or other such heterosexual activities.

As I got older, girls began to be a greater part of my masturbation fantasy. At first I would just think of girls I liked at school and masturbate at the same time. I never really thought of sexual intercourse with girls because I did not understand exactly what interaction you could have with girls.

All I really noticed about having erections when I was seven or eight years old was that they occurred when I thought about a young girl I felt romantically inclined toward. Also, they made it very difficult to roll over in bed. I never knew the purpose of the arousal, but I was aroused.

As I picked up information from peers and the occasional "dirty" book, I began to imagine having sex play and intercourse with the girls in my fantasies. Quite often I would image a "bondage" situation. The girl was often helpless and I would be forcing myself on her. Sometimes I would imagine that I was the captive and the girl or girls were taking advantage of me. I attribute this to my not knowing how to interact with girls or get their attention. So I felt that only by forcing myself on them could I ever have sex.

Upon dating, my masturbation fantasy included the boy I was seeing at the time or images of marriage.

Not all persons who masturbate fantasize. In the Kinsey et al. sample (1953), just about half of the females reported that fantasies had occurred almost always in connection with most of their masturbating, at least during certain periods of their life, with another 14 percent fantasizing some of the time. For a fair number, masturbation fantasies had not begun until some years after they began to masturbate; fantasies were least common for the younger females. For males, 72 percent had almost always fantasized while masturbating and another 17 percent fantasized some of the time. For some, fantasizing is a necessary concomitant of successful masturbating.

I can masturbate only through fantasy; once I lose the dream world I quickly realize how dumb I've been and become very disgusted with my actions. I can only explain this as guilt feelings.

In 1982 Goldman and Goldman published a book on children's sexual thinking. Children in the age range of five to fifteen in suburbs in the English-speaking countries of Australia, England, and North America, as well as children in Sweden, were asked a series of questions, half of which were specifically about sex. A major finding of the study was that in societies where children are deprived of honest answers and explanations about sexuality (which is more or less the case in all of the English-speaking countries), children construct explanations about biological and sexual processes in the form of myths of their own making. Their low-level thinking was conveyed to them primarily as a result of their parents' modesty training. Goldman and Goldman called it low-level thinking because evidence from the Swedish sample indicated that the same retardation was not prevalent in Sweden, where cultural and educational experiences equipped children to understand complex biological concepts. The myths that children deprived of accurate sexual information used in explaining biological processes grew out of the kinds of experiences and education they had received. Goldman and Goldman described three bases for the children's mythologies—the digestive fallacy, analogic teaching, and artificialist explanations. The digestive fallacy (Freud's cloacal theory) was found to be strongly held by younger children. It involves explaining the origin of babies by reference to the digestive system. Children explain that the mother eats food and becomes fat. The food is the baby and it comes out where waste from food normally comes out, through the anus. Goldman and Goldman postulated that myths resulting from retardation of sexual thinking are partly due to inadequate communication and adult inhibitions about using correct terminology and descriptions with children. Many of the analogies used in children's books and by parents to explain the origins of babies, for instance, appear to be taken so literally by young children that they retard rather than advance children's understanding, especially if the analogies are false analogies. The following is a case in point. An interviewer asked a young child, "If I asked you to tell me just one way that people get babies, what would you say?" The young child answered, "I would say, a store, buy a duck, and a duck. . . . I saw it in a book. . . . [F]ind out from this book" (Bernstein and Cowan 1975:87). In other words, the analogy used in the children's book apparently left the child with the impression that to get a baby one needed a duck, perhaps several ducks!

New medical artificialist myths have replaced older artificialist myths reflecting the power and mystique associated with doctors, nurses, hospitals, and operations today and the secrecy that often surrounds them. Artificialist myths that are strongly held by children in their early years involve not any biological functions but rather what goes on in hospitals.

Goldman and Goldman (1982) claimed that a fairly recently developed medical myth is that of conception and birth by Cesarean, in which children tell, or at least perceive that they have learned, about the mother being cut open to insert a baby and later cut open again to take the baby out. The significantly higher level knowledge of sexual processes that Swedish children possess is reflected in less mythological explanations. (See also Barthalow-Koch 1980.) For people who believe that knowledge is better than ignorance, even for young children, this is compelling evidence.

REFERENCES

Ames, L. B. "Children's Stories." *Genetic Psychology Monographs* 73(1966):337–96.

Barthalow-Koch, P. "A Comparison of the Sex Education of Primary-aged Children in the United States and Sweden as Expressed through Their Art." In *Childhood and Sexuality*, edited by J.-M. Samson, 345–55. Montreal: Editions Etudes Vivantes, 1980.

Bernstein, A. C. and P. A. Cowan. "Children's Concepts of How People Get Babies." *Child Development* 46(1975):77–91.

Borneman, E. "Progress in Empirical Research on Children's Sexuality." *SIECUS Report* 12(1983):1–6.

Conn, J. H. and L. Kanner. "Children's Awareness of Sex Differences." *Journal of Child Psychiatry* 1(1947):3–57.

Gardner, R. A. "Sexual Fantasies in Childhood." *Medical Aspects of Human Sexuality* 3(1969):121, 125, 127–28, 132–34.

Goldman, R. and J. Goldman. *Children's Sexual Thinking*. London: Routledge and Kegan Paul, 1982.

Kanner, L. "Infantile Sexuality." *Journal of Pediatrics* 4(1939):583–608.

Martinson, F. M. "Child Sexual Development and Experience: What the Experts Are Telling Parents." Paper presented at the Society for the Scientific Study of Sex annual meeting, November 1992.

Pitcher, E. G. and E. Prelinger. *Children Tell Stories: An Analysis of Fantasy*. New York: International Universities, 1963.

Ramsey, G. V. "The Sexual Development of Boys." *American Journal of Psychology* 56(1943):217–33.

Roiphe, H. and E. Galenson. *Infantile Origins of Sexual Identity*. New York: International Universities, 1981.

Rosenfeld, E. L., R. Huesmann, L. D. Eron, and J. V. Torney-Purta. "Measuring Patterns of Fantasy Behavior in Children." *Journal of Personality and Social Psychology* 42(1982):347–66.

Wermer, H. and S. Levin. "Masturbation Fantasies: Their Changes with Growth and Development." *The Psychoanalytic Study of the Child* XXII(1967):315–28.

6

Sexual Encounters with Older Children, Adolescents, and Adults

In the process of growing up, it is almost inevitable that a child will have one or more encounters of a sexual nature in which the other party is either too young or too old to be regarded as a peer. Most of these encounters are accidental and incidental in the life of the child. Gagnon (1965), in reanalyzing Kinsey data on encounters of females who as girls had had encounters with an adult male, found that the first and largest group was composed of persons reporting single events of a clearly accidental nature usually with a complete stranger. A second group of accidental cases consisted of those who reported multiple accidental contacts, but with different men, in different circumstances, and with the events fairly widely separated over time.

There are many cases of someone exposing himself or herself to a child, encounters wherein the one who initiates the exposing is an older child, a preadolescent, or an adolescent. There are more occasions of this type of sexual encounter than there are encounters involving children and adults. For example, the ages of the female partners of the preadolescent boys who participated in sexual encounters in the Ramsey (1943) study were in 80 percent of the cases within one year of the same age as that of the boy; in 11 percent of the cases the girls were two or more years older; and for the remaining 9 percent the partners were two or more years younger. The girls involved were usually neighborhood friends, female relatives, girls met during family visits, females of the same family, and occasionally an older girl or woman. Since the preadolescent or adolescent who initiates a sexual encounter with a child is usually known by the child and by the child's parents, he or she dare not be too aggressive and often feels the need to be devious because of the danger of being detected, embarrassed, and perhaps punished. Sometimes the child exposes herself or himself at the instigation of the older person.

> The very first sexually related experience I remember was with another girl. When I was four or five, this older neighbor girl once enticed me with an offer of money to remove my panties and pull up my skirt in her presence. This experience was purely exhibitory, as there was no bodily contact between us. The inquisitiveness on her part helped to strengthen an already growing feeling in me that the genital area was "special" in some way and should not be shown to others since she felt it necessary to get my consent. However, at this age, it did not seem inappropriate to me that another girl would be interested in my genitals.
>
> This happened when I was about ten. Two sisters who lived next door and I [a boy] used to play in my playhouse. We'd sit and tell spook stories. One day the older sister, who was probably fifteen, made a bargain with me. She would show various parts of her body if I would show mine. I agreed. She then exposed her breasts. But when it was my turn I became too embarrassed to show a girl my penis and ran away. From then on both girls refused to play with me.
>
> When I was seven years old my parents asked a thirteen-year-old boy to come and "sit" with me while they went out. I went to bed. He got on top of the covers next to me. After trying to sleep I turned around to tell him to quit squirming because I couldn't sleep, when I noticed his pants were unzipped and his penis was out. Being a seven-year-old, I bluntly told him that that was not nice and that he'd better get off my bed.
>
> My first acquaintance with sex was in second and third grade when I began to talk with older boys and girls because of my early maturation. The older children told me that girls had a hole between their legs called a "cunt." They told me to look at a cunt as soon as possible. Well, curiosity had been invoked in me, so I stripped the girl next door and looked at her.
>
> Several times when I was young it seemed as if exhibiting my body in the presence of another boy would be exciting. I remember one situation in particular with a boy three years younger than I; I was about seven years old at the time. We were both wearing swimming

suits, but were walking together at some distance from the beach. I openly fondled myself to the point of erection and then displayed my penis to the younger boy. Then I urged him to pull down his suit also, but for some reason he refused. Yet he was not at all subtle at looking at my erect penis.

Sexual encounters often involve an adult male exposing his genitals to one or more children, especially girls, without their being any physical contact between them. In some cases the exhibitionist also masturbates in their presence. It is not uncommon for children who grow up in urban environments to encounter such exhibitionists. A child, especially one who has had a sheltered upbringing, may find the experience upsetting.

The darkness of the theater made us [seven-year-olds] a little reticent to search for a seat until our eyes readjusted to the indistinctness. To my right sat two of my friends and next to one friend sat a man. He was no concern of ours because many times parents accompanied their children to the movies. What happened then took place so quietly and swiftly I doubt that anyone else in the theater was aware of the horrible sensation that we felt. All of a sudden I was aware that my friends were not watching the movie, but their attention and eyes were focused on the man. His raincoat was open and he had fully exposed himself and was manipulating his genitals. He seemed to be almost laughing softly, and sat there staring at us. We did not fully understand what was happening. We sat there and stared in awe with feelings of curiosity and inquisitiveness while greatly mixed with emotions of distaste and repulsiveness. Yet, we did not scream or break into hysterics, but sat as though we were hypnotized. We must have all felt as though the sight was wrong, because in unison the three of us quietly left our seats and headed towards the back of the theater.

When I was very young, maybe seven or eight years old, I got to know an old couple who lived next door. I never really liked the man though, because he was hunched over and always seemed a little friendly, especially when his wife was gone. One day my friend and I were supposed to take something over to the neighbor lady, but the lady wasn't home and only the old man was there. He was friendly to us as usual and gave us candy. Then he told us that he had something special to show us, but we had to promise not to tell anyone what we saw. Of course we were curious, so he took us in the bathroom, unzipped his pants and showed us his pubic hairs, saying that they were about the longest ones anyone could have. We were really shocked and left immediately. I don't think that I was so scared by what happened as by what could happen if anyone found out.

Touching and fondling of a sensual and sexual nature are experiences that children can have with persons of almost any age. Some are accidental or incidental to other activity; some are pleasant to the child, others are not.

I do recall that I had pleasurable experiences connected to the rectal portion of a physical examination given me by the doctor during one illness when I was about three.

In first grade, I can remember my first actual erection. I was sitting on my teacher's lap. I was neither ashamed nor embarrassed at the little bulge in my pants.

Children seek body contact with others. In one survey, kindergarten teachers reported that children often sought to be held close, to sit on the teacher's lap, and to be kissed. In another survey, the majority of teachers reported that the major motivation of the children appeared to be to experience security, closeness to an adult, and affection; 20 percent reported that in some instances the child explored the teacher's body (as reported by Reinisch 1987). Many times the touching or fondling involves a child having contact with someone only a few years younger or older for security, out of curiosity, or for pleasure.

When I was about seven years old, my eleven-year-old neighbor girlfriend and I would get together and play games which involved fondling and exploring each other's body. A game that we played was referred to as "upper" and "lower" and this would include choosing one of the words and the other person would stimulate that portion of the body for about ten to fifteen minutes. This we did anywhere since it did not involve taking off clothes, just placing the hand inside the clothes. By sexual contacts I had a release of strange feelings inside me and got much physical satisfaction when arms were holding me.

I [a twelve-year-old male] was curious about the little girls' genital system and I proceeded to suggest a game where I could explore this area. We turned off the lights and I played the role of monster. The other children were to run around the room and keep away from me. When I caught them I would supposedly eat them. The game went fine and I achieved what I had set out to do—to find out what a girl's "penis" felt like when I squeezed it. As the children ran from me I would catch a boy and throw him down and pretend I was eating him and give him a little hit on the rump or on the leg, but when I caught a little girl I immediately grabbed her vaginal area with my whole hand and rubbed and squeezed it a couple or three times. While I did this I distracted her attention from my grip by mumbling a few monster groans and yelling "I'm going to eat you."

From my kindergarten year, there is one incident which stands out in my mind. My sixteen-year-old uncle was baby-sitting while my parents were out for the evening. After I got ready for bed he asked me if I wanted a back rub, I said yes, and I laid down on the bed. He rubbed my back and after a few minutes he pulled down my pants. He told me not to say anything and proceeded to examine and finger my genital area. He said that he just wanted to see something. I don't exactly remember my reaction although I know I was too embarrassed to tell my mother.

There was an older boy who lived on our block who initiated sexual contact with me. He was about fifteen years old and I [a girl] about ten, I believe. He used to tease us and play school with us. Whenever he'd punish me he'd take me into his little room behind the furnace and pretend to whip me. One time though he put his hand down my pants. I got scared but he convinced me it was all right to do. From then on he would put his hand in my pants whenever an opportunity presented itself. He even started putting my hand in his pants to play with his penis. Once he baby-sat with me and brought a friend. I enjoyed their attention and obliged them in sex play. They took me into my room separately and showed me their penises and had me fondle them. I remember thinking that they were huge. This type of activity continued with these two for about four months. I was getting very upset about my relations with these boys and decided to call it all off. I was beginning to change to conform to our society's standards.

I think I found out about intercourse and conception from an older neighbor boy [probably about three years older]. He would give me pornographic books and magazines to read, and when he had a chance, would fondle my body some. This was happening when I was about in sixth grade.

The older of the two does not have to be much older to impress the younger partner and win compliance, as in the following case.

He came and sat down next to me at the party, put his arm around me and kissed me, at the same time putting his hand on my breast. Since it had been arranged that I was to be with him, and since I assumed that this was as accepted as was kissing, I did not resist. It was important to me that he was interested since he was a year older than me, and therefore would be quite a status builder. We spent this evening together, he quite fascinated with my breasts (he told me I had quite a handful), but this was the extent of the sex play. We were never together again, nor did we even ever acknowledge that we knew each other upon meeting.

It is not unusual for a child to be touched or fondled by an older man, often a grandfatherly figure well known to the child, a man who takes the child into his lap and tells stories or reads a book. For young children there is a greater likelihood of such an encounter with an older man that they know than there is that an older stranger will expose himself to them.

"Grandpa" (my aunt's father), who was about eighty-five years old, piled the three of us on his lap to read us a story from a children's book. At age seven, I still enjoyed having older people read to me. After he finished reading he placed the book on the coffee table and just talked with us about what we had been doing. As he was talking, I felt his aged hand reach into my underpants and touch me. I was pretty young so I really didn't know what to do or say. I felt like telling what he was doing, but I was too afraid so I remained completely silent.

Our next door neighbors had their grandfather living with them, whom I had admired very much for the stories he told. One day while sitting on his lap, he started rubbing my genitals. I tried to make an excuse to leave, but he would not let me. I was scared. Finally, I broke away from the old man. This happened every time I would visit there until I refused to go into the house anymore.

Sexual encounters with someone older often prove to be a learning experience. Boys in particular, and especially those from lower socioeconomic classes, receive considerable information and "help" on sex matters from older boys, or from adults, and in many cases their first heterosexual experience is with older girls who are already experienced (Kinsey et al. 1948). Rainwater (1970) found that preadolescents in the Pruitt Igo area of St. Louis, a federal slum, showed a great interest in the grown-up world. These preadolescents observed adolescents engaging in sexual activity since much adolescent sexual activity took place outside the home—in hallways, stairwells, galleries, laundry rooms, and on the project grounds. Adults in Pruitt Igo thought of preadolescence as a period of intense imitation of adults, unlike middle-class adults, who are more likely to think of their children as innocent of such knowledge and activity. Children were often present during conversations about sexual behavior, a favorite topic of conversation among both adolescents and adults. They learned the words, concepts, implications, and meaning of sexual terms and could appear remarkably sophisticated even though they had not had exposure to sexual behavior directly. One of the ways that their sexual knowledge developed was through learning to master traditional stories or "toasts" of the folk culture. Actual observation of sexual activity made it possible for many preadolescents to tell stories abut such events. By preadolescence they not only knew "how to do it" but they also knew that sexual activity is regarded as desirable. According to Rainwater, they moved early and easily from listening to sex conversation and from passive observation to active participation. Not that they moved directly to sexual intercourse; their relationships were primarily social and were modeled after the "going steady" pattern of youth. Play activity often eventuated in playing at sexual intercourse, which may or may not involve actual penetration. The girls were ambivalent about playing sex with a boy; however, they were committed anticipatorily to the roles of sex partners as part of their developing conception of themselves as women.

The following cases of middle-class children also have an instructive element.

> I remember one scene very well. He had an older sister. Now that sex was beginning to interest me, I wanted to know what his sister was like. In short, I had very little knowledge of girls. He described her very unattractively. In fact, it made me somewhat nauseated to think of a girl in respect to her genitals.

> My first encounter with sex as a reality was when I was about seven or eight. A helpful older friend casually offered me a rather vague definition of coitus. I wasn't really at all sure of what he meant. It seemed like a strange thing to do with a girl as the thought had never entered my mind before. There was no desire on my part to learn anything more about it at the time.

> When I was eight years old, a boy at the age of puberty fascinated me with off-color stories which I really didn't understand. Following a few nights of dirty jokes, he proceeded to demonstrate masturbation

to me. When he had succeeded in reaching orgasm, he suggested that I try like stimulation. There were no results in my efforts whatsoever.

My cousin [age 13] and I [age 10] would lie on the couch, unzip each other's pants and fondle, caress and masturbate each other. We would take turns stimulating each other and then fondle each other simultaneously. I received great pleasure from this.

When I was approximately nine years old I played with a 14-year-old boy. One day when we were out in the woods he unzipped his pants and began to masturbate. I didn't really know why. He told me that it just felt good, that it was fun, and I should try it. So I did, and it was fun. I masturbated by myself following this episode. I also masturbated with the neighbor boy, not performing the act on each other but being in the same room together.

Boys sometimes engage in fellatio with older boys or men.

When I was eight years old a boy at the age of puberty enlisted my aid in forming a "club." Each meeting had to be brought to order by rubbing the blunt edge of a knife along each other's penis. Following this we engaged in fellatio, for him to orgasm, for me there was no apparent purpose.

One day the adolescent boy who taught me how to masturbate told me what a "blow job" was and wanted me to give him one. I made a feeble attempt at it but I thought it tasted awful.

Among the Siwams of Africa, all men and boys engage in anal intercourse. Males are singled out as peculiar if they do not indulge in these same-sex activities. Prominent Siwam men lend their sons to each other, and they talk about their masculine love affairs as openly as they discuss their love of women. Both married and unmarried males are expected to have both same- and opposite-sex affairs. Among Aborigines of Australia, this type of coitus is also a recognized custom between unmarried and uninitiated boys (Ford and Beach 1951). Among the Aranda of Australia, pederasty is a recognized custom. Commonly a man who is fully initiated but not yet married takes a boy ten or twelve years old who lives with him as a wife for several years, until the older man marries. The boy must belong to the proper marriage class from which the man might take a wife.

Anal intercourse is not a common children's activity in America, but it does enter into the sexual practice of some. In the following case, a boy of five or six is introduced to both oral and anal sex, as well as to mutual masturbation.

My first sexual experience with another boy came at the age of five or six, when I would play with this boy who was about sixteen. He would ask me if I wanted to go into his house for something to eat, like some cookies or something. Of course I would go. Next he would ask me if I would go into the bedroom with him. Upon entering the bedroom, he would undress and ask me to do the same. I would, probably out of fright. After undressing, he would tell me to bend over and then he would insert his erect penis into my anus and start thrusting back and forth. He would then stimulate my penis and want me to do the same to him. We also masturbated each other, with him reaching orgasm and myself only being stimulated. I also spent some time in oral-genital contact. I did find the whole experience quite pleasing and continued to engage in these activities for a week or two. Then, and I don't recall why, we suddenly stopped doing it completely.

I [eleven years old] had become friendly with a boy five years younger than myself and soon started thinking of sex. We began by fondling each other's genitals and soon proceeded to playing games involving our sex organs. This relationship went on for a month; we attempted to engage in penile-anal intercourse.

Sexual intercourse is not a common form of sex play in which children in U.S. society engage, while it is established practice in some societies. Among the Lepcha of India, older men occasionally copulate with girls as young as eight years of age (Ford and Beach 1951). This is not regarded as a criminal offense. Girls in Basutoland, South Africa, are expected to attire themselves with rings or braided grass and cowhide, and white clay is rubbed on their bodies and legs. These young girls are first instructed for a period of some weeks in the details of sexual intercourse, after which they are circumcised (that is, the clitoris is amputated). This is done to prevent them from engaging in promiscuous sexual activity when they are married. As part of this rite, they act out coital positions with each other (*Sexology* XXX, 1964).

Among preadolescents in other societies—the Moari of New Zealand, the Trobrianders of Melanesia, the Chewa of Africa, and the Lepcha of India—it is common for girls and boys to be active participants in full sex relations several years before puberty and in some cases much earlier. In permissive societies, there may be active instruction in sex matters by older members of the group (Ford and Beach 1951).

In most societies, adults are active in trying to prevent children and preadolescents from having sexual encounters rather than initiating them into such encounters. In some societies, adults attempt to deny young children any form of sexual experience or sex education. In the past this was the prevailing practice in many homes in the United States. Many adults avoid mentioning matters of sexual significance in the presence of children. Among the natives of the western Carolines, sex is never discussed in the presence of children, especially girls. Cuna children of Panama remain ignorant of sexual matters, as far as adult instruction is concerned, until the last stages of the marriage ceremony. Chagga of Tanganyika children are told that babies come out of the forest (Ford and Beach 1951). In a number of these societies, particular pains are taken to prevent offspring from accidentally observing sexual behavior.

One method of controlling the sexual activity of children is to separate the sexes and keep them under surveillance. Among the Murgen of Australia, boys are removed from the family dwelling to the boys' house or bachelors' house when they are four or five years old; this is done for the specific purpose of preventing them from witnessing sexual behavior at home. The Panamanian Cuna children are not even allowed to watch animals give birth (Ford and Beach 1951).

Among the Abipone of South America, boys and girls are strictly segregated at all times and premarital chastity is said to be universal. A similar situation exists among the Arapaho, Cheyenne, and Papago of North America, and Wapisiana of British Guiana, all of whom keep the sexes strictly apart from childhood. Boys and girls never associate in the absence of chaperones (Ford and Beach 1951).

In the United States, parents, the church, the school, courts, and other agencies are influential in defining and controlling sexual behavior. For example, the school—grade school, junior high school, high school—is permissive in that it plans dances and parties for boys and girls, but chaperonage is commonly provided and erotic behavior is proscribed. The schools take a proprietary interest in the total life of the students and are sometimes more restrictive than are parents.

But communities in the United States vary greatly. Kinsey et al. (1948) found that interest in coitus and knowledge and acceptance of premarital coitus were well established among boys age seven in some American communities, and in some instances as early as four years of age. Especially in some urban communities, by age seven boys knew that coitus was one of the activities that most of their older acquaintances were engaging in; and they had already learned that coitus was one of the things considered highly desirable. Much of the sexual sophistication came from associating with older companions. Children overhear adolescent boys talking to one another about naked women and couples who have had sex relations. The size and shape of a woman's vagina are topics of conversation among boys and men, and younger boys learn from older males that women are objects of sexual gratification. As a consequence, they orient their thoughts and behavior in accordance with what other males expect of them as young, on-the-make machos. Kinsey et al. (1948) found that boys from comparatively sheltered upper socioeconomic level homes were not exposed to such experiences and were likely to confine their sex play to exhibition and manual manipulation of the genitals. These boys did not attempt coitus because, in many instances, they had not learned that there is such a possibility. In spite of their limited contact with coitus or information about coitus, children raised in homes of educated parents have often seen adult genitalia at an early age, primarily because of the greater acceptance of nudity in their homes when compared to the homes of others.

The following cases show some of the naiveté present in sexual encounters between children and someone older.

My [a girl] earliest experience with sex occurred when I was approximately five years old. One day a buddy of my brother's came over who was eleven years old. My brother was not home at the time so he asked if I would play with him. I said I would. Somehow we ended up in the haymow sliding around in the hay. Later, resting on top of the hay, he asked me if I wanted to play doctor. Thinking it was all in fun, I said yes. He informed me that he was the doctor and I the patient. I was about to have a baby and he was going to operate. He unzipped my pants, took them off, and proceeded to do the same with his. He tried to have intercourse but did not succeed. Thinking it all was a game, and of course knowing nothing about sex at that time, I thought it was perfectly all right.

In the following case a girl eight years old and "not very mature" was with her cousin, age sixteen, who was "sort of left with the responsibility of baby-sitting."

He had me undress in his room and he began to fondle me and investigate the various unfamiliar parts of my body. Then he laid me on the bed and he also took off his clothes before lying down on the bed with me. He continued to caress me and soon became quite excited and then he attempted to have intercourse with me, but the pain was too great for me and I began to cry, and there was also some bleeding in the vaginal area. I ran to the bathroom and stayed there crying until my parents returned a short time later. When my parents returned my cousin was hysterical and running around gathering clothes and food in preparation for running away from home. The calm and reasonableness shown by my parents saved the day for both of us.

In the following case involving urethral damage, the sexual naiveté of the two middle-class boys is apparent.

We two boys, I age seven and my friend twelve years old, came from middle-class families having many interests in common, such as baseball and hiking. Sex, however, was not one of these interests for me as it was for him. I cannot exactly remember how it all started, but I think it was in the form of the "doctor" game. He fondled my genitals and encouraged me to do the same to him. It was a new experience for me, but I cannot recall if it was pleasurable or not. His erect penis was quite a mystery to me, and I had no idea of why it got that way. At one time he was quite rough with my penis and as a consequence there was some blood in my urine. This frightened me, but it seemed to frighten him more when I told him that I was going to tell my mother. Since he was older than I was and one of the few playmates that I had, I did not tell.

It is widely held that children would be better able to deal with or avoid sexual encounters of the kind discussed in this chapter if age-appropriate sexuality education was generally available to them. We discuss the issue of sexuality education in Chapter 7.

Most of the studies of child sexual activity wherein the participants have been of markedly different ages have dealt only with clinical or offender populations, and few studies have sought any but the negative reactions of children to these sexual experiences—thus giving a distorted view of reality (Kilpatrick 1992). The clinical samples consist almost exclusively of those suffering relatively serious negative consequences with 20 to 25 percent of the cases of suspected child–adult sexual abuse showing signs of physical trauma or injury. The recent study by Kilpatrick (1992) differs from other studies in that it includes no clinical or offender population and allows for respondents to give positive and neutral, as well as negative, responses to their childhood sexual experiences. The sample population was 501 Southern adult women who were asked to recall their childhood sexual experiences. Sixty-seven percent of the white respondents and 36 percent of the black respondents reported having sexual experiences as children. Kilpatrick found that the larger proportion of women (67%) remembered having participated voluntarily rather than involuntarily in sexual activity, and most reported having been active in initiating such activity, while a smaller proportion (33%) felt that they had in some way been pressured or forced. Thirty-eight percent of the women found their experiences to be pleasant, 37 percent neither pleasant nor unpleasant, and 25 percent found the experiences to be unpleasant. Sixty-eight percent reported having had overall positive responses to their sexual experiences, while negative reactions of anger, fear, or shock were reported by 32 percent. Despite the negative responses, 72 percent felt that their child sexuality was not harmful, and 83 percent felt it was not abusive. The women had had partners in their sexual experiences as children who were relatives and nonrelatives, as well as older and younger. Most women had had their sexual experiences with other children; only 17 percent of the white sample and 5 percent of the black sample reported having had partners who were at least five years older than they were. Like Kilpatrick, Goldman and Goldman (1988) found in a retrospective study of 1,000 Australian youth that most had either positive or neutral feelings regarding their childhood sexual experiences, and most of their experiences had been with children their own age.

The type or age of partners did not appear to be significantly related to the women's functioning as adults, which challenges a linear assumption that all children are victimized by any type of sexual experience with a person who is five or more years older (see also Constantine 1981b).

The sexual activity engaged in was "kissing and hugging in a sexual way" (37%) followed by exposing of the genitals. The only other activity that 5 percent or more had participated in was masturbation. Only 2 percent had engaged in intercourse by age fourteen or younger.

Despite these findings of little reported harm or abuse from their childhood sexual experiences, Kilpatrick (1992) warned that under no circumstance should her findings be used to sanction child–adult sexual relations. Kilpatrick agreed with Finkelhor (1979) that a child is not in a position to give informed consent, and such relationships involve unequal power on the part of the participants. Kilpatrick concluded that in child–adult sexual activity there is psychological, if not physical, coercion and it should be treated as such.

The question of child sexual activity being abusive remains a moot question in U.S. society. There is no universally accepted definition of child sexual abuse and no general agreement about the effect on children of sexual experiences with persons somewhat older. Evaluations of child sexual experiences vary. Some use sex abuse as a catchall term for almost any type of child–adult contact. Others see any experience as abusive if the older participant is at least five years older than the child (Finkelhor 1979).

Furthermore, there is to date no consensus on the scope of child–adult sexual activity or the emotional and behavioral consequences for the child (Konker 1992). Even the professional groups involved in dealing with individual cases of child sexual abuse differ in their definitions. Each tends to use definitional criteria that are most in line with the goals of their profession (Haugaard and Reppucci 1988). There is increasing agreement among social workers and other helping professions that sexual abuse of children does involve coercion or nonconsensual sexual acts (Kilpatrick 1992).

The term *child abuse* was not used before the 1960s, and its definitional reach has expanded in the years since. Broadening the definition of the terms *child abuse* and especially *child sexual abuse*, after the initial paper by Kempe and associates (1962) on the "battered child syndrome" and the widespread attention it received in the media, was due to several factors. First was concern for the well-being of children, though there is to date no consensus on what constitutes sexual well-being for children. Second, child advocates felt that it was important to alter and broaden the consciousness of children about what constitutes abuse. The child, or the adult whom the therapist suspects may have been abused as a child, often has a definition of sexual abuse that does not include what was done to him or her, as was true in many of the cases in which children talk about their experiences; therefore the therapist feels it is incumbent to ask about specific behaviors and feelings that the therapist regards as indicative of abuse (Hunter 1990). It stands to reason that the broader the therapist's definition of what constitutes sexual abuse, the more abuse the therapist will find. According to Gilbert (1991), another reason for broadening the definition of the term *child sexual abuse* was to persuade the public that the problem is vastly larger than was commonly recognized. And it has worked; a broader definition has alerted both professionals and the public to the prevalence of child sexual experiences that should be defined as abusive. Only one in ten Americans thought that child abuse was a serious problem in 1978, in contrast to nine out of ten by 1982 (Gelles and Straus 1988). A recent poll of mental health and legal professionals in Virginia shows that 20 percent of them believe that frequent hugging of a ten- or fifteen-year-old child by his or her parents requires intervention. Most of the professionals felt that no intervention was necessary if a parent often kissed a five-year-old on the lips, but from 44 to 67 percent felt some intervention should be undertaken if ten- or fifteen-year-old children were kissed. Similarly, 90 percent felt that some type of intervention was called for if a parent often appeared nude in front of a ten- or fifteen-year-old child, and 75 percent if the child was five years old (Haugaard and Reppucci 1988).

In a detailed review of nineteen studies concerned with the prevalence of child sexual abuse among females, the results ranged from a low of 6 percent to a high of 62 percent of all females reporting abuse (Peters, Wyatt, and Finkelhor 1986). Such statistics reflect differences in definitions of child sexual abuse used in various studies, different populations surveyed, and differences in questions asked of the sample population.

The field of child sexuality is in its infancy as far as defining what is abusive and in identifying, preventing, and treating sexual activity that is abusive. The efforts that are being made by institutions and professionals need to be supported, while at the same time efforts to increase our knowledge base and efforts to address the need for uniform standards of training, supervision, intervention, protocols, counseling and therapy, evidence collecting, and civil and criminal court testimony need to be pressed forward (Konker 1992).

A family needs to be close. An infant, especially, needs to feel accepted and attended to by its parents and to feel closely identified with them (Bowlby 1965). Giovacchini (1986) referred to this primitive form of erotic need and preoccupation embracing the need to be cared for, fed, nurtured, and comforted as pregenital. Freud also ascribed sexual feelings to young children, referring to these early sexual feeling as pregenital in contrast to genital sexual feelings that occur with gonadal maturation (Brill 1948). Meeting the infant's attachment needs does not need to include fondling and stroking the stomach, stimulating the child's genitals, passionately kissing on the lips, or performing fellatio on a male infant. These and other practices have been found to occur among incestuous mothers (Chasnoff 1986; Stroufe and Ward 1980). Such behaviors are seductive. They are insensitive and unresponsive to the real needs of the child and draw the child into patterns of interaction that may be overstimulating and inappropriate; the infant primarily needs affectionate care and nurturance (Sroufe and Ward 1980). On the other hand, it is important that overt erotic attraction and gratification occur in the parent–child relationship, but it is important that it be regulated by the family (Parsons 1954).Dysfunctional families are often dysfunctional in that they evince too much interconnectedness and enmeshment, or homeostasis (Alexander 1985).

Genital eroticism is both permitted and expected of the marital pair and, in a well-regulated home, they are considered to have a monopoly on the right to genital eroticism. Pregenital eroticism, on the other hand, is approved in the early mother–child relationship and also in the father–child relationship. Strong motivation is built up in the child through the enjoyable erotic relationships. The extent of the erotic involvement and its control is the parent's responsibility. Without such control the parent–child relationship, in fact the family sexual culture, will become incestuous. Finkelhor (1978) distinguished three dimensions of family sexuality that are determinative. First, families may prompt positive or negative attitudes in their children toward sexuality. In sex-positive families, children receive accurate information about sex and are given positive attitudes about their bodies and shown physical affection, while in sex-negative families sex is fraught with anxiety and taboos. The second dimension concerns how sexualized the family interaction becomes. In highly sexualized families, members use one another as sexual objects, while low sexualized families discourage sexual activity inside the family. The third dimension involves personal boundaries. Clear boundaries imply respect for the privacy of each member of the family, with a clear differentiation of sex roles between adults and children. With poor personal boundaries, family members intrude on one another, and adult sexual behavior is not clearly distinguished from child sexual behavior. The 1986 World Health Organization report on child sexual abuse describes what it calls an incestogenic family as a family that is socially isolated; the father is often depressive and possessive and tends to sexualize his own problems and his relations with the child or children; the mother often appears to be psychologically submissive and unable to protect the children.

In families wherein a parent becomes sexually involved with a child, it is most often an experience involving father and daughter. Summit and Kryso (1978) asserted that

> a father should be harmless for his daughter to flirt with. He should approve, admire, and respond to her growing sexual attraction and should provide a controlled, self-limited prototype of the sensual experiences she will develop with other men later on. Both father and mother should share this sense of appropriateness of the father–daughter prototype romance, and both should be comfortable in recognizing and defining appropriate limits. (Summit and Kryso 1978:123)

In such a relationship incestuous activity begins only if and when the father bends these limits and the mother does not interfere. When a father interacts with his daughter, he may at first have no intention that it shall be sexual, but there is a body of clinical evidence that shows that incestuous desires are regularly engendered within the nuclear family and are kept in restraint only through persistent individual repression and social pressure. There does not appear to be any natural revulsion against incest in young children. The impression is gained that fathers are often "careful seducers," cunning in their attempts to persuade a child of theirs and able to break down any resistance with a high degree of success (Frude 1982). Sexual behavior between father and daughter is often marked by a gradual escalation from fondling and petting to more specifically genital behavior. One daughter reported that she enjoyed it and was fully orgasmic in the relationship (Frude 1982); Renshaw (1977) reported that twenty-two of thirty-two male and female sons and daughters climaxed in such father–child sexual relationships.

It has been said that children are easy to seduce because they want to be seduced. This is true if by that we mean that infants and small children want to be held and caressed, or as Bowlby (1965) has said, the drive of the organism toward achieving good personal relations is real and persistent. And if they have learned that sexual behavior is a way to gain attention of a parent, such behavior may become pronounced as they curry attention. This does not imply that the child recognizes the sexual meaning of his or her behavior in any adult sense, nor does it attribute culpability to the child in any ensuing incestuous activity that an adult may initiate. The child uses it instead to obtain nurturance (Rosenfeld 1979).

Some families claim to practice family sexual expression in a highly educated, sophisticated, and carefully responsible manner with benefit to their children (Nelson 1979). There are those among them who have been influenced by Wilhelm Reich, René Guyon, and others, and they are convinced that they have a responsibility to help their children express their infantile sexuality in a genital way (Miller 1984). Such behavior leaves many questions, however. Are not nurturing and affectionate intimacy sufficient to socialize children into this later sensual aspect of life? Will children from such families continue to feel that sexual intimacy in the family was right and good for them? Will they subsequently be able to establish satisfying sexual relationships with others beyond the home? For now at least, a more conservative course of action appears to be more prudent for the family.

Father–daughter incest receives a great deal of attention in the media and is by far more frequently recorded both clinically and in court records, but sibling sexual activity is thought to be much more common. Siblings, especially those who are close in age, spend much time interacting with each other during the growing-up years. They live in the same household, are constantly present, and share space, toys, clothes, and the attention of their parents and of each other.

The emphasis in the literature on sibling interaction has been largely limited to consideration of only one dimension, namely, sibling rivalry. But sibling interaction includes much more than just rivalry. Abramovitch et al. (1982) observed children from two-child, middle-class, suburban families, following them from approximately one and a half years old until the older sibling was approximately five or six years old. They found that for intervals as long as three years, siblings spent a great deal of time interacting with each other. They were deeply involved with each other, regardless of the age intervals between them or the sex composition of the pair. They treated each other in aggressive ways, but they also cooperated, helped, and acted affectionately to each other. In other words, they demonstrated a full range of social interaction. The authors concluded that sibling relationships have something in common that is different from other relationships, "perhaps closer, deeper, more automatic and spontaneous" (Abramovitch et al. 1982:84–85). Tsukada (1979), in a review of the literature on sibling interaction, found as well that concentrating on rivalry hides the richness and variety of experience that is sibling interaction. Tsukada concluded that sibling relationships "provide a child in most families with companionship, affection, and understanding, and fulfill needs for peer group association. Furthermore, sibling associations are lifelong, and in many cases provide significant relationships in adult life" (Tsukada 1979:232). It has been said that the degree of affection between siblings as adolescents is second only to the mother–child tie.

Given the constant, close, intimate interaction of siblings, it is understandable that a certain amount of sex play occurs between them. Some of it grows out of their great liking for each other, as the following cases illustrate.

> I was 8 or 9 and my brother was 10. We were playing in a relatively secluded place, the sun was shining, and we undressed almost completely. He suggested that we lie down. Without objection (I always used to obey him), I did. He had something in mind; he was sexually excited. I did not feel anything sexual, but I was flattered that he wanted to play with me and excited that he wanted to be intimate with me. He performed sexual intercourse with me, but stopped after some minutes. Then we got up and went on as usual.

My brother is a year older than I am. We were very fond of each other. When I was in seventh grade we got very sexually involved. He told me all about sexual intercourse. Every day after school we would go to his room and talk and fondle one another. He had some rubbers and asked if he could have sexual intercourse with me. I almost let him do it, but it was painful. He was very gentle and he said he wouldn't do it. Sometimes we would play rape and I would be in his room and he'd run in. We would fight and finally he'd rip my clothes off. This was one of our favorite games.

My first erection having to do with sexual activity occurred around age 7. I was sitting on the floor in the living room next to my sister, four years older, who was lying face down. The next thing I did was to mount myself on her buttocks and do what would now be called "humping." Our parents were in the room also, but all I cared about was deriving pleasure for myself. My sister complained that I was hurting her, and my parents scolded me a little. I remember being upset at their anger and their embarrassment and confusion when I asked what I did wrong. I didn't do it again when my parents were around but when my sister and I were alone, I would try "feeling good." In such cases, she had to literally fight me off and I'd retreat and do something else. This happened only 3 or 4 times.

But, alas, not all sibling sexual play is so innocent or remembered pleasantly, especially if there is a marked difference in ages between the siblings.

I was a "victim" of incest (not including coitus) with my oldest brother for several years starting approximately at age 8. I lived in constant fear that I would be left alone in the house with him. I hated him with all my heart. I felt I was the only young girl that this ever happened to and, therefore, I had much guilt and never told anyone about it.

Mary was a sixth grader when she was raped by her 16-year-old brother. It was clear that the father, as well as the brother, was a source of sexual torment to her. [A social worker]

There is a special category of adults who enter into the lives of some children; we designate them pedophiles. the word *pedophile* is made up of the prefix *pedo*, which means "child," and the suffix *phile*, which refers to an affinity for or loving. Hence the term *pedophile* literally means "one who loves children." The literal opposite of a pedophile would be a pedophobe, one who fears or hates children. If this were the generally accepted meaning of *pedophile,* we would expect that pedophiles would be highly regarded in our society, but they are not because the kind of love referred to includes sexual love. Pedophiles are more descriptively defined as adults who are exclusively, or primarily, sexually attracted to children; hence pedophilia is defined as a sexual perversion. Pedophilia has to be defined as deviant behavior because there is no room in the normative structure of U.S. society for this form of behavior (Mohr 1981). This normative perspective is reflected in Finkelhor and Araji's (1986) sweeping definition of pedophilia as any adult sexual contact with a child, regardless of motive. There is some difference of opinion about how pedophilia should be defined. A World Health Organization report (1986) states that pedophilia may or may not result in child sexual abuse and should not be used synonymously with child sexual abuse. Pedophiles sometimes defend themselves, saying that their feelings are not exclusively sexual but include interest in how children feel and think (Sandfort and Everaerd 1990).

Sandfort (1982) interviewed twenty-five Dutch boys who were located through their adult partners. The boys were between the ages of ten and sixteen and were involved in a pedophilic relationship with an adult male at the time they were interviewed. The affairs had lasted between two months and six years. Pedosexual contacts usually involve a relatively low level of physical intimacy, such as touching, fondling, and exhibiting, and in the Sandfort study the adult always masturbated the boy; in seven cases the adult had oral-anal contact with the boy; if there was penal-anal contact, the boy most frequently penetrated the man. Almost all of the boys seemed to be heterosexually oriented and though they liked the man, they were not sexually attracted to him. The findings do not support the idea that these boys were seductive children who made the first sexual initiation. In addition, almost every boy recognized that having sexual relationships as a child with an adult is deviant, and since such contacts are also criminal offenses in the Netherlands, it was necessary to keep them secret. Most of the boys had pleasant relationships with their parents. They did not appear to feel coerced into continuing the relationship. I the face of all of this, why did the boys continue their pedophilic relationship? Their motives, aside from the sexual pleasure they received, appeared to be that the boys and the pedophile did lots of things together; the boys were attracted by the atmosphere at the pedophile's place; he was someone with whom they could talk easily; they received support in solving problems at home or in school; they learned from the pedophile or experienced him as a model; and they received from the pedophile friendship and, in a few cases, love. In reacting to Sandfort's findings, it is well to keep in mind that the average Dutch child appears to be more knowledgeable about sexuality than is the average child in the United States.

One cannot generalize from Sandfort's study of twenty-five boys, and cases of violent physical sexual abuse as a result of adult–child sexual relations are extensively documented. Abel, Mittelman, and Becker (1987) reviewed reports from 232 men (guaranteed confidentiality), who revealed that on the average they had victimized seventy-six children. Incarcerated offenders also reported a high incidence of encounters, reporting on the average eleven more victims than those for which they were prosecuted. Whether or not the adult was a "true" pedophile is largely irrelevant; using the term *sexual abuse*, which is derived from a legal perspective, the adult is always the offender and the child is the victim. In more than half of the pedophilic cases the sexual crime was committed many times with the same victim. From this perspective 100 percent of Sandfort's sample of twenty-five boys were victims of sexual crime. The child psychiatrists Brant and Tisza (1977) prefer the term *sexual misuse*, a term that derives from a mental health perspective. They define sexual misuse as exposure of a child to sexual stimulation inappropriate to the child's age, level of psychosexual development, and role in the family. What Brant and Tisza object to, as have other scholars and therapists, is that the term *child sexual abuse* is pejorative and compels one to think only in terms of victims and offenders.

One hears talk about rings, sex rings, or vice rings in which a number of adults are involved with children in illicit activities. Ennew (1986), who was commissioned by the English Anti-Slavery Society to write a report on child prostitution and pornography, had the task of sifting through many reports on vice rings and traffic and has no doubt that some cases exist, but she saw none that were proven conclusively. On the other hand, Burgess (1984), in a two-year project on the use of children in pornography funded by the National Center on Child Abuse and Neglect, reported on fifty-five sex rings in the United States. The methodology used in collecting the information is not discussed in the study and complete data were not available; hence Burgess suggested that the evidence should be treated a primarily descriptive and only possibly indicative of the population of sex rings. Three types of sex rings are delineated in the book. In solo rings an adult operates alone with a small group of children, who know each other and are conditioned or programmed by the adult to provide sexual services in exchange for a variety of psychological, social, monetary, and other rewards. Next is the transition ring. In such rings multiple adults are involved sexually with children and the children are usually pubescent. The adults exchange or sell pornographic photographs of the children and try to pressure the children, who have been tested for their role as prostitutes, into the next level, the syndicated ring. The syndicated ring is a well-structured organization that involves the recruitment of children, the production of pornography, the establishment of a network of customers, and the delivery of trade items (that is, children, photographs, films, and tapes). Ennew (1986) agreed that there is a market for young children and that organized prostitution of children and young people takes place in many countries and in various forms, but she suggested that it is not as large a trade as moral crusaders would wish us to believe.

According to Paul Knuckman (Burgess 1984), children in sex rings come from families from which they are disengaged. They may see the adult in the ring as a surrogate parent and often do not perceive themselves as victims, confusing as they may love, trust, and comfort with sex. Whether or not they experience physical abuse and trauma, they are defined as victims for they are prematurely introduced into adult sexuality and aberrant behavior.

Child pornography is generally defined as magazines, books, photographs, videotapes, and films that depict children of either gender in sexually explicit acts, including exhibition of genitals, masturbation, oral sex, sexual intercourse, and bestiality. Much of child pornography depicts an adult involved with a child in mutual exhibition or some other type of sexual act. Before the late 1960s, adult women with girlish figures were used as models in so-called child pornography; the actual use of children as models, some as young as three years old, is a fairly recent development. Today many authorities believe that a significant number of child pornography "stars" start out as teenage runaways. In one county 86 percent of children involved in child pornography or prostitution were runaways or missing (Burgess 1984). The total number of children involved in child pornography may not be as large as believed since the same children are often filmed or photographed and shown in more than one product of the pornographic media (Ennew 1986). Child pornography is a relatively lucrative business, and children on the street who must be concerned about their survival may find that they are able to earn more from allowing themselves to be photographed or filmed than they can from prostitution.

Unscrupulous adults interested in involving children in some sexual activity often show them pornography as one of several ways used to lower their inhibition and to persuade them to enter into some type of sexual act. Of the sex rings reported on by Burgess (1984), 62 percent showed pornography to the children.

It has been estimated that in the United States 600,000 boys and girls under sixteen years of age engage in prostitution to help supplement their income while on the run (Pierce 1984). It is not so much that sexual abuse at home leads to prostitution as it is that sexual abuse may lead to running away, and running away leads to prostitution. The majority of child prostitutes were runaways; the average age of first sexual intercourse was twelve, with the greatest frequency occurring between ages ten and thirteen (Burgess 1984). A number of children help support their families by working as child prostitutes.

In sum, the sexual encounters of children with older children, adolescents, and adults can be instructive and pleasant, but it can also introduce children into aspects of sexual life for which they are not physiologically, psychologically, or socially ready, experiences that can prove to be exploitative, abusive, and destructive. Children need to be educated in such a way to prepare them for the sexual life they are entering and to protect them, insofar as it is possible, from experiences that are not in their best interest.

REFERENCES

Abel, G., M. Mittelman, and J. Becker. "Sexual Offenders: Results of Assessment and Recommendation of Treatment." In *Clinical Criminology: The Assessment and Treatment of Criminal Behavior*, edited by M. H. Ben-Aron, S. J. Hacker, and E. D. Webster. Toronto: Butterworth, 1987.

Abramovitch, R., D. Pepler, and C. Corter. "Patterns of Sibling Interaction Among Preschool-age Children." In *Sibling Relations*, edited by M. E. Lamb and B. Sutton-Smith, 61–86. Hillsdale, N.J.: Lawrence Erlbaum Associates, 1982.

Alexander. P. "A Systems Theory Conceptualization of Incest." *Family Process* 24(1985):70–88.

Bowlby, J. *Child Care and the Growth of Love*, 2nd ed. London: Penguin, 1965.

Brant, R.S.T. and V. B. Tisza. "The Sexually Misused Child." *American Journal of Orthopsychiatry* 47(1977):80–90.

Brill, A. A. *Lectures on Psychoanalytical Psychiatry*. London: J. Lehmann, 1948.

Burgess, A. W. (ed.). *Child Pornography and Sex Rings*. Lexington, Mass.: Lexington Books, 1984.

Chasnoff, I. J., W. J. Burns, S. H. Schnoll, K. Burns, G. Chisum, and L. Kyle-Spore. "Maternal-Neonatal Incest." *American Journal of Orthopsychiatry* 56(1986):577–80.

Constantine, L. L. "The Effects of Early Sexual Experiences: A Review and Synthesis of Research." In *Children and Sex: New Findings, New Perspectives*, edited by L. L. Constantine and F. M. Martinson, 217–44. Boston: Little, Brown, 1981b.

Ennew, J. *The Sexual Exploitation of Children*. New York: St. Martin's, 1986.

Finkelhor, D. *Sexually Victimized Children*. New York: Free Press, 1979.

Finikelhor, D. "Social Forces in the Formulation of the Problem of Sexual Abuse." University of New Hampshire Family Violence Research Program, 5(1978):1–21.

Finkelhor, D. and S. Araji. "Explanations of Pedophilia: A Four Factor Model." *Journal of Sex Research* 22(1986):145–61.

Ford, C. S. and F. A. Beach. *Patterns of Sexual Behavior*. New York: Harper, 1951.

Frude, N. "The Sexual Nature of Sexual Abuse: A Review of the Literature." *Child Abuse and Neglect* 6(1982):211–23.

Gagnon, J. "Female Child Victims of Sex Offenders." *Social Problems* 13(1965):176–92.

Gelles, R. J. and M. A. Straus. *Intimate Violence: The Definitive Study of the Causes and Consequences of Abuse in the American Family*. New York: Simon & Schuster, 1988.

Gilbert, N. "The Phantom Epidemic of Sexual Assault." *The Public Interest* 103(1991):54–65.

Giovacchini, P. L. "Promiscuity in Adolescents and Young Adults." *Medical Aspects of Human Sexuality* 20(1986):24–31.

Goldman, R. and J. Goldman. *Show Me Yours! Understanding Children's Sexuality*. Victoria, Australia: Penguin, 1988.

Haugaard, J. J. and N. D. Reppucci. *The Sexual Abuse of Children*. San Francisco: Jossey-Bass, 1988.

Hunter, M. *Abused Boys: The Neglected Victims of Sexual Abuse*. Lexington, Mass.: D. C. Heath, 1990.

Kempe, C. H. and others. "The Battered-Child Syndrome." *Journal of the American Medical Association* 181(1962):17–24.

Kilpatrick, A. C. *Long-Range Effects of Child and Adolescent Sexual Experiences*. Hillsdale, N.J: Lawrence Erlbaum Associates, 1992.

Kinsey, A. C., W. B. Pomeroy, and C. E. Martin. *Sexual Behavior of the Human Male*. Philadelphia: W. B. Saunders, 1948.

Konker. C. "Rethinking Child Sexual Abuse: An Anthropological Perspective." *American Journal of Orthopsychiatry* 62(1992):147–53.

Levine, M. J. "Pediatric Observations on Masturbation in Children." *Psychoanalytic Study of the Child* 6(1957):117–24.

Miller, A. *Thou Shalt Not Be Aware: Society's Betrayal of the Child*. New York: Farrar, Straus, Giroux, 1984. (Originally published in German 1981.)

Mohr, J. W. "Age Structures in Pedophilia." In *Adult Sexual Interest in Children*, edited by M. Cooke and K. Howells, 41–54. London: Academic, 1981.

Nelson, J. "A View Toward Normal, Healthy Incest." *CSC Nusletter* V(1979):4–6.

Parsons, T. "The Incest Taboo in Relation to Social Structure and the Socialization of the Child." *British Journal of Sociology* 5(1954):101–17.

Peters, S. D., G. E. Wyatt, and D. Finkelhor. "Prevalence." In *A Source Book on Sexual Child Abuse*, edited by D. Finkelhor, 75–93. Beverly Hills, CA: Sage, 1986.

Pierce, R. L. "Child Pornography: A Hidden Dimension of Child Abuse." *Child Abuse and Neglect* 8(1984):483–93.

Rainwater, Lee. *Behind Ghetto Walls: Black Families in a Federal Slum.* Chicago: Aldine, 1970.

Ramsey, G. V. "The Sexual Development of Boys." *American Journal of Psychology* 56(1943):217–33.

Reinisch, J. "The Kinsey Report." *Minneapolis Star and Tribune* January 29, 1987, 15D.

Renshaw, D. C. *Sexuality Today* 1(1977):4.

Rosenfeld, A. A. "Endogamic Incest and the Victim-Perpetrator Model." *American Journal of Diseases of Children* 133(1979):406–10.

Sandfort, T. *The Sexual Aspect of Pedophile Relations.* Amsterdam: Pan/Spartacus, 1982.

Sandfort, T.G.M. and W.T.A. Everaerd. "Male Juvenile Partners in Pedophilia." In *Handbook of Sexology VII Childhood and Adolescent Sexuality*, edited by M. E. Perry, 361–80. Amsterdam: Elsevier, 1990.

Sroufe, L. A. and M. J. Ward. "Seductive Behavior of Mothers of Toddlers: Occurrence, Correlates, and Family Origins." *Child Development* 51(1980):1222–229.

Summit, R. and J. Kryso. "Sexual Abuse of Children: A Clinical Spectrum." *American Journal of Orthopsychiatry* 48(1978):237–51.

Tsukada, G. K. "Sibling Interaction: A Review of the Literature." *Smith College Studies in Social Work* 49(1979):228–47.

7

Sexuality Education

Physiological, psychological, and social factors all contribute to the forming of one's sexuality. Every day of life, a child learns something about what it means to be sexual, how he or she is defined by others, how one should act, what is expected of one. In every society, children from birth are placed within a division of society according to their physiological sexual features. Hence, it is biologically determined sex, not socially defined sex, that determines one's basic sexual status; for all gender systems take their justification from physiological distinctions between female and male, and from birth on a person learns the social rules that influence and determine sexual behavior for that gender within the society. Every person a child meets throughout the day, every agency, the media, as well as institutions that have a direct stake in doing so—family, school, state, church—contribute to shaping the child's sexuality. What children have traditionally learned in U.S. society is that they are not to engage in any activity that is sexual in nature. In a classic study conducted thirty-five years ago, Sears, Maccoby, and Levine (1957) showed how mothers, the primary teachers of infants and children, follow out a path of avoidance of anything that might be thought to permit, encourage, or interpret any child activity as sexual in nature.

In the past, parents, school, and church have done little to provide adequate, age-appropriate sex instruction for children. The following case indicates a child's reaction to the teachings of the church.

> For a 4- or 5-year period, beginning when I was 10 years old, I became extremely aware of sex taboos via the church. I'd hear stories about

God's love including God's loving decree that anyone who had had and engaged in sex was a sinner.

An overriding rationale for limiting children's access to knowledge about sexuality and the sexual practices of adults was to protect them. American society was not unlike most of the restrictive societies that maintain a public conspiracy against the acquisition of sexual knowledge by children (Ford and Beach 1951). The cult of innocence through keeping children ignorant developed and strengthened in Western society toward the end of the last century to the point that the difficulty of talking about sexuality to children appeared to be almost natural (Elias 1978/1939). The restriction may have developed in part as a defense against advances in awareness of the sexual life of children represented in theories of Sigmund Freud and others.

The cult of innocence was easiest to maintain in middle-class communities where the sexual proclivities of children were regarded as premature if not aberrant. In economically poor and overcrowded inner-city communities, childhood sexual innocence was almost impossible to maintain. As Rainwater wrote in *Behind Ghetto Walls* (1970), adults in a slum area had come to regard the sexual interests and activities of children as natural, if lamentable. Older children learned fully developed conceptions of sexual behavior and of its desirability through talk and observation.

Many things motivate children, even at a very early age, to gather more information than their parents think they should have about many things concerning sexuality. Examining their own body parts; noticing the differences in body parts of girls and boys; experiencing feelings in the pelvic area that they do not understand; the presence of a new puppy in the home; seeing the birth of a litter of kittens; noticing the changes in a pregnant relative or neighbor; overhearing a chance bit of conversation about some aspect of sexual life; as well as any discrepant event provokes prolonged attention leading to understanding or anxiety, can be the motivator. Children up to around eight years of age demonstrate an ease with sexual topics. They appear to respect others of their age, both boys and girls; are able to talk about sex with interest and mutual consideration; and comfortably discuss words like *uterus*, *breasts*, and *penis* (Brick 1985) though they do not use those Latin-derived terms unless these have been taught by adults.

Repressing sexual knowledge and experience has effects other than keeping children naive and innocent. Denying information leaves the control of children's sexuality in the hands of adults. Without names for the sexual organs and terms for sexual activity, children's fantasy tends to overrun their sexual life; they are also likely to identify the sexual organs with excretory functions.

The following two cases relate to the practice of restricting information given to children or giving words without factual information. In the first case, a ten-year-old girl related that she had been reprimanded by a parochial day school teacher for using the word *sex* and that she had been "morbidly afraid of falling in love" because her parents had told her that a person got pregnant only when married and in love. She concluded that at the end of her home and church "sex education" she, at age thirteen, "was a cold unemotional adolescent who valued virginity above all else. However, my inability to relate to boys was a constant source of frustration." In the second case,

> I would not talk to mother about private and important matters. She had not volunteered information and I dared not ask for it. My knowledge of sex was very shallow and warped. When I began menstruating, I cried hysterically, not so much at the sight of the blood, but at the prospect of having to tell my mother.

According to the therapist Helen Kaplan (1974), restrictive upbringing is an extremely important and highly prevalent source of conflict that leads to sexual alienation and dysfunction. Children who are not instructed must rely on each other's experiences and bits of information they find.

Naming something is an essential process in relating to the object named; the name expresses the person's attitude and it determines that attitude. Once named, the object can be singled out, classified, and made available. The unnamed object is always the unknown whose relation to the person cannot be clarified (Wrage 1969). Or, as one student puts it,

> The sexual education I received was very slow coming, and very impractical. I could have been spared many a thought and such if properly educated at an early age. Curiosity is one of man's biggest strengths and weaknesses. If it is satisfied quickly, one can move on. If it is not, you spend many a wasted hour in contemplation of simplicity.

From day one in the life of their child, parents are giving messages about sexuality whether or not they are conscious of it and whether or not they mean to. If they do not provide information, they still create attitudes and orientations through which information received from other sources will be filtered. Many parents attempt to hide any aspects of adult sexuality.

My parents even seemed a little embarrassed when they kissed in front of us and showed little outward expressions of love. I cannot even remember seeing them hug. This bothered me when I was growing up.

Children often test their parents regarding sexual knowledge and sometimes find their parents wanting.

I can remember asking my mother what p.g. meant and she replied "pretty girl." I was testing her. Another question that was never answered correctly was "Mommy, do you get pregnant by taking a pill?" to which her reply was "Yes."

I believe that you just can't take your parents for truth in these matters. Perchance this is what starts a basic gulf or mistrust between many parents and children: that one of the first important issues in your life you take up with parents, they tell you things which do not apply; as a matter of fact, the near opposite of what applies. How apt is a person to seek repeated counsel from those he has seen to be wrong in the past.

Sexuality educators assert that for the child to develop a healthy sexuality as he or she matures, the encouragement and/or explicit training of sexually appropriate behaviors is required. Children need to be made aware of their own sexuality; this requires that their mentors accept sexuality from a developmental perspective and encourage developmentally appropriate behavior.

Children remember being warned or scolded about sex.

The first real scolding I received for touching or playing with my penis was when I was four or five years old. I was in the bathroom and my father walked in. I had worked up a soapy lather all over my crotch. He scolded me and told me not to do that again. Misunderstanding the chastisement to be not merely for playing with my genitals but for washing them too, I was afraid to wash myself for a long time.

When I was around three or four I must have seen someone masturbating. I tried it too and felt very proud of what I had learned and the strange sensation it aroused. I excitedly showed my mother; she was shocked. She told me not to do it anymore and spanked me. Then she never mentioned it again. I was stubborn enough to continue because I enjoyed the feeling.

My friend, another girl, and I decided to ask my mother about the funny sensation we had both experienced while lying in bed at night.

She gave a vague explanation, but it was nothing more than a warning not to do it again. This planted in my mind that talk about the body was bad and only had dirty connotations. I slowly became quite self-conscious about my body.

After I had bathed, my mother was examining me to see if I was clean or not. As she cleaned my navel, I had an erection. She said "Oh Gary!" and gave it a little slap. It just frightened the sexual dickens out of me.

Two experiences are fresh in my memory. When I asked my mother where the kittens came from and why they couldn't go back there again, she scolded me and said nice little girls don't ask things like that. Later I heard older kids use the word "fuck" in a dirty story. I asked my mom what the word meant. She didn't explain but rather warned me that the next time I used the word I could expect to get my mouth washed out with soap! How I made it through those years I will never know.

In homes where children cannot get satisfactory answers from their parents, an older sibling sometimes comes to the rescue.

Once our family was out for a ride and my brother, who was about 8 years old, asked, "If babies are in mother's stomachs, how do they come out?" Neither of our parents gave him a direct answer, which made me angry. I tried to explain to him the best I could. Another time he used a nasty word for sexual intercourse in talking with me. He knew what it meant, but I told him that he shouldn't use the term in public. I gave him the correct terminology for it.

In my home, I was the one who told my sisters about everything. Mother had always been overly modest. Some very informative books, which I went to on my own for answers, had straightened me out.

The greater acceptance of children as sexual beings in the last two decades and the increase in books and articles for parents of young children would be expected to improve the at-home sexual education of children (Martinson 1992). Since mothers spend the most time with young children, most reactions to at-home instruction is to something involving mother. The following cases give the flavor of some of the positive reactions of children to what they experienced about sexuality in their homes.

I think that I knew more about sex than most of the children my age. My mother informed me at an early age. She always told me things about sex in advance so I never learned anything from the other kids that I hadn't already heard. I have always respected my mother a great deal for this freedom and honesty.

I would say that 95 percent of my sex education has come from my mother. She has told me in such a beautiful way that sex hasn't become dirty and bad in my eyes. I realize how fortunate I am when I hear of girls whose mothers never told them a thing.

The next case comes close to being an ideal daughter–mother relationship as far as communication is concerned.

My mother and I have always had very good communication. We have been extremely close, and we have talked over everything about sex. I think we have helped each other tremendously in understanding each other's generation and their values.

Sex instruction on those less frequent occasions when it is given by fathers is also appreciated if it is done well.

On the way home from shopping my mother said to dad that she had forgotten to buy sanitary napkins. Naturally I asked what they were. Mom and dad looked at each other and said, "Well I think it's about time we tell her." When we got home dad showed me a book of diagrams of the female and male reproductive system. He explained what happened during menstruation and all the rest having to do with reproduction. At first I was shocked to think my parents would do such awful things. The more I asked, the more I realized that it must be a pretty natural process. I think that this matter of fact, down to earth way of explaining has always made it easier to confide in my parents. I have never had to look for information outside of the home.

My formal sex education from my father came when I was in the 5th grade. We had very little difficulty with terms and his explanations using correct terms were very easy to understand. I became aware that the male produces sperm, which are carried by semen, and that I could expect to have nocturnal emissions as I grew older. Even though he didn't go into the mechanics of masturbation, he left me with a feeling that the pressure build-up was normal and that it was nothing shameful if it was relieved. Even though much of the information was given in an unemotional technical language, I was aware that the joys of the act were a part of love and marriage. My father also explained the menstrual pattern of girls and told me that sometimes their emotional make-up is changed during their period. He stressed the feeling of love and respect for others as well as the physical and technical aspects of a sexual relationship.

Parents often receive mixed messages from child guidance authorities regarding how to deal with nudity in the family (Martinson 1992). In the following two cases, children show their appreciation of nudity as part of their at-home sexuality education.

> My parents didn't feel it was necessary to shield our eyes from their bodies nor from the bodies of anyone in our family. Thus, the physical differences between the sexes were made very apparent to me at a very early age.

> I was brought up with the notion that sex and bodies are something beautiful and enjoyable. I would say that my sex education began when I was a baby, if you regard naked bodies as such. Up until I was four years old, we would bathe together at least once a week: my father, mother, and my sister would have water fights in the bathtub as long as there was any water. These sessions got rarer as I and my sister grew; the bathtub simply became too crowded. It wasn't until I started school that I discovered that the genitals were something you should giggle and blush over.

Children appreciate love, respect, and values they learn as part of sexuality education at home.

> My family is a person-centered family. My mother would always say to me, "You are not the only one in the family. There are four others." My parents taught me very early the attitude of acceptance, respect, and desire for other people.

> Even though there is not a "blubbery" show of affection between my parents, it has always been very obvious that they were very much in love. I was especially aware that this relationship was indeed a happy and desirable one.

> I was brought up in a family which did not set limits and make decisions for me. My parents always explained to me their values and standards but have not imposed them on me. I have set my own standards and adhere more strictly to them than I would were they imposed. I respect my parents a great deal for allowing me the right

of individual choice and decision. Because of this I have freedom of communication with them. Never have I felt the "generation gap."

Historically, children in America got the bulk of their sexual information, such as it was, through associating with their peers. The following are reactions to sex "instruction" from peers.

One day one of my girl friends told me what one of the words meant, that is, how babies were made. She made the situation seem very horrible, and I felt very sick about it. She teased me because we were four children in my family and she was the only child in hers, which meant my parents were much worse than hers.

About the age of eight, I was walking with a friend who all of a sudden blurted out, "You know, when your penis gets hard, that means you want a mate." I was rather taken aback by this statement because I saw no connection between a hard penis and getting married.

It was in the locker room that I first began to pick up things about sex. I would hear older boys (9th graders) talking about a specific girl and someone would ask "Does she give?" I would ask myself "Give what?" When I finally figured it out, with the help of a few friends, I still thought that you urinated in her vagina.

During sixth grade a group consisting of me, another girl, and three boys met in the hall during breaks to discuss sex and related topics. One boy in particular always had a sexual "fact" or two to impart to us, such as how far a penis had to go into a girl to get her pregnant. We didn't giggle or squirm during these discussions. We were inquisitive but not embarrassed.

Many parents assert that they are ill equipped to give sex information to their children because they are confused as to what they ought to teach them, at what age they ought to teach them, and how they ought to teach. Help for parents is becoming more available. In the last decade, a number of books of guidance for parents have become available, books written by sexuality educators and therapists. Most parents want their children to have sexuality education in school. In the United States, twenty-two states require it and twenty-four states encourage it, yet only an estimated 10 percent of children receive comprehensive school-based sexuality education (Scales 1986). Fewer than one in six of the state curricula provide young people with a comprehensive base of information and education on sexuality before they leave the twelfth grade. Most sexuality education programs in the schools do not begin until the junior or senior high school years, and few of them address sexual issues comprehensively.

Parents in a high socioeconomic suburb of an eastern U.S. city were asked to rank their preferences regarding the inclusion of a number of topics in a sexuality education program for sixth graders (Silverstein and Buck 1986). A number of sensitive topics were included. The approval rates they received are as follows: child molestation, 81 percent; sexual attraction, 80 percent; intercourse, 79 percent; venereal disease, 74 percent; rape, 73 percent; birth control, 71 percent; exhibitionism, 71 percent; masturbation, 66 percent; abortion, 63 percent; homosexuality, 63 percent; and pornography, 56 percent. Thirty-two percent approved of including the advantages of premarital sex, but a larger percentage (69%) supported the inclusion of the disadvantages of premarital sex. Comments of parents focused on the need to include responsibility for behavior and moral issues regarding sexual intimacy. Several noted that it was not the nature of the topic that they disagreed with but the age at which it is appropriate to discuss sexuality.

Croft and Asmussen (1992) attempted to identify the ideal time for the introduction of various sexual topics, using a community survey in a predominantly middle-class, Midwestern metropolitan area. Of thirty-four topics mentioned, mothers believed that all of them needed to be initiated prior to high school graduation, and mothers, along with the family life educators, agreed that twenty-one of the thirty-four topics ideally should be introduced in the elementary school grades rather than in higher grades. These included reducing fear and guilt regarding sexuality; how sexuality development affects personal growth and development; information on male and female genitalia; biology of human growth, reproduction, and birth; development of interpersonal skills with the opposite sex; encouraging students to talk with parents regarding sexuality; correct physiologic myths; biological changes at puberty and lifespan development; pubertal experiences similar for peers; and AIDS education. Mothers and educators also thought the following subjects, which were never introduced in the school, should be introduced in middle school: information about abnormal sexual development; abortion information and abortion's effects on the body; integrating family values into discussions; and contraceptive information. Both also agreed that the topics of venereal disease, sexually transmitted disease, and abstinence, which were already introduced at the middle school level should continue to be offered there.

The aforementioned studies show clearly that there is parental support for comprehensive sexuality education beginning as early as the elementary grades.

A task force of leading health, education, and sexuality professionals developed *Guidelines for Sexuality Education: Kindergarten–12th Grade* (1991). The task force spelled out what it regarded as appropriate developmental messages that should first be discussed at each of four stages of development—ages five through eight, nine through twelve, twelve through fifteen, and fifteen through eighteen.

Some of the topics that the task force recommended be discussed with children in early elementary school, ages five through eight, and upper elementary school, ages nine through twelve, include the following:

Body Parts and Functions

Each body part has a correct name and a specific function. (5–8)

Boys and men have a penis, scrotum, and testicles. (5–8)

Girls and women have a vulva, clitoris, vagina, uterus, and ovaries. (5–8)

Like other body parts, the genitals need care. (5–8)

Individual bodies are different—sizes, shapes, and colors. (5–8)

Male and female bodies are equally special. (5–8)

There are no jobs that are only for boys or only for girls. (5–8)

At puberty, boys begin to ejaculate and girls begin to menstruate. (9–12)

Early adolescents often feel uncomfortable, clumsy, and/or self-conscious because of the rapid changes in their bodies. (9–12)

During puberty, many people begin to develop sexual and romantic feelings. (9–12)

Human beings have a natural physical response to sexual stimulation. (9–12)

Children are not ready for sexual intercourse. (9–12)

All people are sexual beings. Exploring feelings about sexuality is common. (9–12)

Masturbation is often the first way a person experiences sexual pleasure. (9–12)

Masturbation does not cause physical or mental harm. (9–12)

Touch

Both girls and boys have body parts that feel good when touched. (5–8)

Boys and girls may discover that their bodies feel good when touched. (5–8)

Some boys and girls masturbate. Others do not. (5–8)

Masturbation should be done in a private place. (5–8)

Everyone, including children, has the right to tell others not to touch their body when they don't want to be touched. (5–8)

No adult should touch a child's sexual parts except for health reasons. (5–8)

Sexual abuse occurs when an older, stronger, or more powerful person looks at or touches a child's genitals for no legitimate reason. (5–8)

If unwanted or uncomfortable touching happens, the child should tell a trusted adult. (5–8)

If a stranger tries to get a child to go with him/her, the child should leave quickly and tell a parent or other adult. (5–8)

A child is never at fault if an adult touches him/her in a way that is wrong or uncomfortable. (5–8)

Most adults and adolescents would never abuse children. (5–8)

Both boys and girls can be sexually abused. (5–8)

Sexual abuse is most often committed by someone known to the child. (9–12)

Appearance, Friendship, Dating, Commitment

People can have many friends. (5–8)

There are different kinds of friends. (5–8)

Friends are either male or female. (5–8)

When two teenagers or unmarried adults spend their leisure time with one another, it is often called dating. (5–8)

Teenagers and adults often have several romantic relationships. (5–8)

Before people commit, they should be friends, spend time together, and get to know one another well. (5–8)

During puberty many people begin to develop sexual and romantic feelings. (5–8)

Love means having deep and warm feelings about one's self and others. (5–8)

It is not known why a person has a particular sexual orientation. (9–12)

A bisexual person is attracted to men and women. (9–12)

Homosexual, heterosexual, and bisexual people are alike except for their sexual attraction. (9–12)

Homosexual love relationships can be as fulfilling as heterosexual relationships. (9–12)

Gay men and lesbians can form families by adopting children or having their own. (9–12)

The value of a person is not determined by their appearance. (9–12)

Many skills are needed to begin, continue, and end friendships. (9–12)

Friendships are necessary for most people to feel good about themselves. (9–12)

Liking yourself enhances loving relationships. (9–12)

Teenagers and adults often have several romantic relationships. (9–12)

Sexually Transmitted Diseases (STDs), Human Immunodeficiency Virus (HIV), Acquired Immunodeficiency Syndrome (AIDS)

People who have not engaged in certain behaviors do not have STD/HIV. (5–8)

A small number of children are born with HIV from an infected mother. (5–8)

A person cannot become infected with HIV by being around or touching someone who has AIDS. (5–8)

To have AIDS means that HIV has done enough damage to the body that serious diseases have been acquired. (9–12)

Parenting

Sexual intercourse occurs when a man and a woman place the penis inside the vagina. (5–8)

Intercourse is a pleasurable activity for most adults. (5–8)

People are able to have babies only after they have reached puberty. (5–8)

Reproduction requires both a man and a woman. (5–8)

People can have children whether they are married or unmarried. (5–8)

Not all men and women decide to have children. (5–8)

All children should be wanted. (5–8)

When a woman is pregnant, the fetus grows inside her body in her uterus. (5–8)

Smoking, drinking alcohol, and using other drugs can hurt a fetus before it is born. (5–8)

Babies usually come out of a woman's body through an opening called the vagina. (5–8)

Some babies are born by an operation called a Cesarean Section. (5–8)

Parenting is an adult job. (5–8)

Parenting can be a wonderful experience. (5–8)

Parenting is a lot of work. (5–8)

Divorce is usually difficult for parents and for children. (5–8)

After a divorce, parents and children continue their lives in a new way and usually become happy again. (5–8)

There are ways to have genital intercourse without causing pregnancy. (9–12)

Sexual intercourse provides pleasure. (9–12)

When a man and woman want to have sexual intercourse without having a child, they can use contraceptives to prevent pregnancy. (9–12)

A legal abortion is very safe. (9–12)

A pregnant woman who does not want a child or an abortion can place her baby for adoption when it is born. (9–12)

People who decide to have children need to provide for them. (9–12)

Men and women have important parental responsibilities. (9–12)

Drugs may affect one's future ability to have healthy children. (9–12)

Values

Different religions may teach similar or different values. (5–8)

Some religions teach that contraception is desirable; others do not approve of contraception. (9–12)

Decisions about having children are based on religious beliefs, cultural traditions, income, and personal wishes. (9–12)

Abortion is legal in the United States. (9–12)

Some people believe abortion is morally wrong; others believe a woman has a right to choose abortion. (9–12)

Sexuality education outside the home for young children is at present only in the early stages of development and implementation. A model for helping early childhood educators develop policies and programs for children's sexual learning has been field-tested in a number of childhood programs by The Center for Family Life Education (Planned Parenthood of Greater Northern New Jersey).

To develop and initiate a kindergarten through high school sexuality education program, it is important that both parents and teachers be informed about and have an opportunity to discuss sexuality as a developing human capacity that begins at birth and continues. This must be done as a beginning phase of a developmental stage in a community or school program of sexuality education, during which the appropriate goals are identified for each grade level (Croft and Asmussen 1992). Parents, teachers, and others in the community would all need a voice in deciding at what age topics in *Guidelines for Sexuality Education: Kindergarten–12th Grade* should be introduced in the curriculum and how they should be taught.

In the United States, all states at present either require or recommend HIV and AIDS education, and all states stress sexual abstinence; but only eleven states provide balanced information on safer sex and abstinence. Abstinence has been the primary emphasis for as long as sex education has been offered in the schools. There is concern today that emphasizing mainly abstinence and the negative outcomes of sexual activity—pregnancy, HIV/AIDS, and STDs—gives children an unbalanced perspective on human sexuality; we must also fear the fear of sex. More parents and educators are speaking out in favor of a balanced perspective within the context of an accepting and positive view of human sexuality. To date only three states present HIV/AIDS information within a context that emphasizes both the positive and negative consequences of sexual activity (Britten, de Mauro, and Gambrell 1992), and only five states acknowledge sexuality as a natural part of life and include information on the range of sexual activities and behaviors. Seven of the eleven states providing balanced information on safer sex and abstinence discuss low-risk, noncoital sexual activity.

Sexual intercourse is now normative behavior for American high school students since 54 percent of ninth through twelfth graders and 72 percent of high school seniors have had sexual intercourse (Haffner 1992). We are slowly learning what Sweden, with a much longer history of sex education in the schools, learned some years ago—namely, that telling youth that they should postpone their sexual debut was not enough. Something had to be done to educate about sexual responsibility for those who were or soon could be expected to be sexually active. Since the majority of students in the United States experience sexual intercourse prior to graduating from high school despite the traditional stress on abstinence in sexuality education programs, it is important to include condom information as a preventative measure. This information is given in thirty-seven states. But only five states provide practical information on condom use, such as how to obtain, use, and dispose of condoms (Britten, de Mauro, and Gambrell 1992). Condom instruction appears to be having some effect in the United States, since there has been a positive change in condom utilization among young people (Haffner 1992).

Carefully planned and developed curricula require teachers who are convinced of the importance of sexuality education and who feel competent regarding their own preparation. They also need to feel confident that they have the support of school officials and the community. Before attempting sexuality education, all teachers need opportunities to examine their own learning, experience, and values regarding sexuality, and they need practice using "teachable moments." In the following two cases, the teachers were not prepared to deal sympathetically and sensitively with drawings made by young children.

> As a teacher's aid I worked with a woman who was competent and firm with her second graders. Each day we did art projects to help them develop their imagination. One day they were to draw and color the thing that most impressed them about where they lived. At the end of class the teacher called upon several kids to show their pictures in front of the class. I will never forget the one boy and his picture. He lived on a farm and drew a picture of a cow giving birth. The teacher asked him to explain the blob in the corner and he said it was the afterbirth. A few of the "more worldly" pupils giggled and the others followed

along, but didn't understand. The teacher got so embarrassed that she was very harsh with the boy and made him put his head on his desk.

As a young teacher teaching first grade, I had my pupils working on "season" windows. I asked one boy who was working on the "Spring" window what he had drawn that was spring to him. He told and showed a picture of a "little boy and his penis peeing into the wind outside." My first reaction was a smile and a laugh and a thought that it was pretty natural and original. Then a click went off in my head that I was supposed to be a teacher—should a teacher approve of that? or should a teacher react? None of the children were reacting silly toward it, but I unfortunately decided to interpret his drawing as "dirty" or "naughty." So I said something like, "Tom, do you think you should be drawing things like that?" Immediately after, I realized how silly I sounded. Tom possessed the healthy attitude, whereas I was affected by the "traditional" viewpoint.

Sexual educators have been under attack in communities across the United States for providing sex education to children. In 1990, two states rescinded their mandates for sexual education in response to opposition groups. A large part of the current controversy centers around the changing focus of school sexuality education that has taken place within the last decade (Scales 1986). Prior to that time, sexuality education had focused largely on helping people avoid the negative consequences of sexual decisions that could lead to contracting sexual diseases, unplanned, unwanted pregnancies, school dropouts, early marriage, and a life of poverty. Currently sexuality education deals with these issues but also views sexuality in a positive light. It is argued that a major purpose of public schooling must be to teach children how to reason, to question, and to accept responsibility—*how* to think, more than *what* to think; that public education has an obligation to present a wide variety of ideas that reflect the perspectives of the entire community and address the needs of all pupils (Sedway 1992). On the other hand, there are groups, often referred to as far right or religious right groups, who promote a narrower curriculum that eliminates the discussion of controversial topics (such as birth control, HIV/AIDS, abortion) and focuses exclusively on a program of sexual education that fosters sexual abstinence as the only behavior that can or should be supported both for practical and moral reasons. Though this approach may have the singular support of certain conservative groups, sex-for-procreation that devalues other forms of sexual behavior (such as engaging in alternatives to sexual intercourse for pleasure) also have support in U.S. society. Barriers to comprehensive sexuality education for children and youth grow out of the conflict between those who believe that the next generation should be fully and completely educated on human sexuality and those who do not. A history of repression of open, rational discussion of sexuality has left U.S. society more uncomfortable with the subject of human sexuality than are some other societies. As a result, we are inclined to define human sexuality only in terms of sexual intercourse and school sex education as intervention to prevent the negative consequences of sexual intercourse from occurring too early in life. In other words, we have not distinguished between developing sexuality and reproductive sexuality in our school-based sexuality education. Age-appropriate sexuality education deals with developing sexuality; it has less to do with reproduction. School administrators are reluctant to sponsor sexuality education programs partly out of a desire to avoid religious and political conflict, though studies show that only 1 to 3 percent of parents have refused to have their children participate in such education (Scales 1980). Professionals are also confused about the rapid change in sexual values and lifestyles and how they should proceed in the face of the changes. Due to our failure to perceive the need for sexuality programs and services, we do not have a pool of teachers prepared and comfortable to teach the material. In those states where teachers are mandated by law to teach sexuality education, the teachers usually lack the necessary training and often teach it without confidence or enthusiasm (Krueger 1991).

Focusing on sexuality education, rather than sex education, may appear to the reader to be only a semantic change. But sexuality education broadens the scope, emphasizing that sex focuses attention on behaviors and activities that comprehensive education hopes to postpone. All children in school are developing sexually. They need to have their attention focused on that development. On the other hand, introducing contraceptive instruction comes none too soon since an estimated 30 percent of sexually active adolescents become pregnant during their teen years. Approximately 600,000 of the pregnancies in the United States annually are unintended pregnancies of single female teenagers. Sexually transmitted diseases—gonorrhea, chlamydia, herpes, and cervical cancer—are occurring at high levels in the United States, and adolescents are both the recipients and transmitters of these infections (Fisher 1990). American adolescents, even preadolescents, have been allowed substantial freedom of action but without enough information and guidance in dealing with the powerful sexual feelings that commonly arise around, or even before, puberty. Teenage pregnancies are far more common in countries that restrict or delay sexuality education (such as the United States, New Zealand, and Thailand) than in countries with previously high rates—Sweden and Denmark, for example—that have introduced early and comprehensive sexuality education in schools and have seen ten years of dramatic decreases in the rates of teen pregnancies. Goldman and Goldman's (1982) interview study with children in the English-speaking countries of Australia, Great Britain, and North America, as well as Sweden, found that Swedish children were consistently better informed for their ages, were less inhibited about discussing sexuality, and were better prepared for their adolescent and adult years than were their peers in the English-speaking countries. The responses of the Swedish children provided strong evidence that children have the intellectual capacity to deal responsibly with sexual information if they have been informed rather than uninformed or misinformed. Because the sexuality of children and youth is a developing sexuality, their sexuality education must also be ongoing. One or two "facts of life" talks will not suffice.

All states provide parents with the option to excuse their children from this instruction—this despite fear of the spread of HIV/AIDS. Few parents exercise this choice.

It is important not only that parents be informed about the sexual topics being covered during the school year—they need also to be encouraged to facilitate family discussion about sexuality in the home, for only in the home can such education be integrated into the family's value system. Parents may welcome being directed to educational materials that will increase their knowledge of children's developing sexuality as a way of improving their "askability" in discussions with their children.

REFERENCES

Brick, P. "Sexual Education in the Elementary School." *SIECUS Report* XIII(1985):1–4.

Britten, P. O., D. de Mauro, and A. E. Gambrell. "HIV/AIDS Education." *SIECUS Report* 21(1992):1–8.

Croft, C. A. and L. Asmussen. "Perceptions of Mothers, Youth, and Educators: A Path Toward Détente Regarding Sexuality Education." *Family Relations* 41(1992):452–59.

Elias, N. *The History of Manners*. New York: Pantheon, 1978. (Originally published in Switzerland in 1939.)

Fisher, W. A. "An Integrated Approach to Preventing Adolescent Pregnancy and STD/HIV Infection." *SIECUS Report* 18(1990): 1–11.

Ford, C. S. and F. A. Beach. *Patterns of Sexual Behavior*. New York: Harper, 1951.

Goodman, E. "The Risk in Making Sex a Fearsome Thing." *Star Tribune* (Minneapolis), April 4, 1992, 14A.

Goldman, R. and J. Goldman. *Children's Sexual Thinking*. London: Routledge and Kegan Paul, 1982.

Hacker, S. S. "The Transition from the Old Norm to the New: Sexual Values for the 1990s." *SIECUS Report* 18(1990):1–8.

Haffner, D. "Youth Still at Risk, Yet Barriers to Sex Education Remain." *SIECUS Report* 21(1992):10–12.

Kaplan, H. S. *The New Sex Therapy*. New York: Brunner/Mazel, 1974.

Krueger, M. M. "The Omnipresent Need: Professional Training for Sexuality Education Teachers." *SIECUS Report* 19(1991):1–4.

Martinson, F. M. "Child Sexual Development and Experience: What the Experts Are Telling Parents." Paper presented at The Society for the Scientific Study of Sex annual meeting, November 1992.

National Guidelines Task Force. *Guidelines for Comprehensive Sexuality Education: Kindergarten–12th Grade*. Sex Information and Education Council of the U.S., 1991.

Rainwater, L. *Beyond Ghetto Walls. Black Families in a Federal Slum*. Chicago: Aldine, 1970.

Scales, P. "Barriers to Sex Education." *Journal of School Health* 50(1980):337–42.

Scales, P. "The Changing Context of Sexual Education: Paradigms and Challenges for Alternative Futures." *Family Relations* 35(1986):265–74.

Sears, R. R., E. E. Maccoby, and H. Levine. *Patterns of Child Rearing*. Evanston, Ill.: Row, Peterson, 1957.

Sedway, M. "The Right Takes Aim at Sexuality Education." *SIECUS Report* 20(1992):13–19.

Silverstein, C. D. and G. M. Buck. "Parental Preferences Regarding Sex Education Topics for 6th Graders." *Adolescence* XXI(1986):971–80.

Wrage, K. *Man and Woman: The Basics of Sex and Marriage*. Philadelphia: Fortress, 1969. (Originally published in German in 1966.)

8

Children and the Law

Students of childhood in a number of professions have attempted to trace the history of child paradigms and the accompanying treatment of children within the Western world. A widely held opinion among such scholars is that both the perceptions of children and the treatment of children have improved markedly in the Western world at least from the sixteenth through the twentieth century. Whether there has been such an evolution and such progress in child perception and care is a moot question (Pollock 1983). That there are different perceptions of children and that some perceptions have predominated more at some times than at others is less debatable.

Perceptions of children and of child care come to be reflected both in patterns of behavior and in the law of the land. In this chapter we focus only on one area of law relating to children, namely legal and judicial decisions dealing with child sexuality. Societies not only have general perceptions about the nature of children, they also have specific perceptions about their sexual nature and how, where, when, and with whom their sexuality shall be expressed, if at all. Different scholars, in describing the differing paradigms affecting children and child care, have employed various descriptive concepts.

In dealing with child sexuality, I will use the three descriptive concepts that Lee (1980) employed: property, protection, and personal paradigms.

Reprinted with revisions, from F. M. Martinson, "Current legal status of the erotic and sexual rights of children." In *Handbook of Sexology*, edited by M. E. Perry, 113–24. Amsterdam: Elsevier, 1990. Used with permission.

According to the property paradigm, children are the physical property of adults. Their bodies and their sexual activity are in the power of adults. In extreme cases, the child's body may be mutilated (castration, circumcision, clitoridectomy) or used for sexual purposes by an adult without the child's consent. In milder cases of sexual control, the child may be prevented from or punished for enjoying his or her own body through genital play or masturbation. According to Lee, in the mildest cases of sexual control the child is denied the age-appropriate information necessary to know how to be sexual or is fed misinformation (Sears, Maccoby, and Levine 1957). According to the protection paradigm, the child is a person in training and is held in trust for a period of time until deemed old enough or mature enough to look after himself or herself. From the perspective of a personal paradigm, children are persons and citizens in their own right. From this perspective, age is not considered a more valid basis for discrimination against certain categories of persons than are race, sex, or religion.

According to DeMause (1974), the sexual use of children by adults (the property paradigm) was far more common in the past than it is today. The child in antiquity, both in Greece and in Rome, was likely to be engaged in sexual activity with adults at the adults' discretion. Where homosexuality with free boys was discouraged by law, men were known to have kept slave boys for sexual purposes. According to DeMause, "the Greeks and Romans couldn't keep their hands off children" (DeMause 1974:547). Boy brothels existed in urban centers, and castrated boys were favored sexual partners by men in imperial Rome. Castration of boys was common enough in Rome, for sexual and other purposes, so that during Constantine's administration a law against castrators was enacted.

It was not until the introduction of Christianity in Western society that a conception of children as innocent and as inappropriate sex objects became a dominant cultural paradigm—a protection paradigm. Efforts to dissuade adults from engaging in sexual activity with children continued throughout the seventeenth century, and from the eighteenth century it became common for little children to be discouraged, even punished, for playing with their genitals or masturbating. Close supervision, punishment, restraints, and surgical procedures such as circumcision and clitoridectomy were employed to prevent masturbation (Rachford 1907). From early on, circumcision was recognized as a means of contributing to the control of male sexual passion. Philo wrote in the first century that circumcision was for "the excision of passions, which bind the mind. . . . The lawgivers have commended that this instrument . . . be mutilated, pointing out, that these powerful passions must be bridled, and thinking not only this, but all passions would be controlled through this one" (DeMause 1974:526).

Procedures for controlling child sexuality continued into the twentieth century and included circumcision and a protective and repressive posture toward child sexuality. The protection paradigm, still a predominant paradigm in the Western world, when applied to child sexuality means that a properly raised child shall observe no sexual activity, shall hear no sexual talk, and should not be involved in any sexual activity. A major change in the protection paradigm was instituted in the latter half of the twentieth century, when sex education was introduced in school curricula in Western countries. Sweden was the first country to require comprehensive sex education for all children beginning in the primary grades. Even today, comprehensive sex education for all children beginning in the primary grades is not common practice in all countries in the West (Jackson 1982).

Historically, there has been a change in child sex laws and judicial procedures. According to the Dutch jurist Brongersma, the idea that sex in itself could harm a child was absent in European culture, and hence penal law was silent on the matter until fairly recently. "Children were on equal footing with adults, protected against rape, violence, and abuse of authority, but never against sex as such" (Brongersma 1984:80). This was the situation in the Netherlands up until 1886, for instance. During the nineteenth century, penal codes were extended with a new provision against indecent behavior with children. The concepts of age of consent and statutory rape came into use. Child sex laws have been clearly shaped within the dictates of a protection paradigm.

According to common law (law based on custom and precedent), an infant reached full maturity at twenty-one years of age. The concepts of minority and majority rest on the assumption that children, called infants or minors, are incapable of self-management—management of property, management of their sexuality, etc. Age of minority is a matter of legislative regulation, and hence a status rather than a fixed or vested right, and is subject not only to be fixed by legislative action but also to be changed (Ginnow and Gordon 1978). Today, legal age in the various European, Asian, Latin American, and North American jurisdictions varies from age eighteen to twenty-one. A minor may become emancipated at an earlier age through voluntary, parental, legal, or judicial action in some jurisdictions, and in many countries marriage of a minor is sufficient to bestow legal status.

The crime of statutory rape is defined as rape not necessarily because the younger partner was forced or coerced into engaging in a sexual act or because the young person did not consent to engage in the sex act, but because legally the person was not of the age to have his or her consent recognized by the court. In other words, minors are defined as incapable of giving consent. Societies have struggled with their attempts to determine fixed ages below which a child, though old enough to engage in certain sexual acts and personally mature enough to consent to the activity, is not deemed mature enough to give informed consent to engage in a sexual act. To date no generally accepted age has been determined. In the 1800s in England the age for statutory rape was as young as ten years; today the age is sixteen, with physical rather than chronological maturity used to justify leniency or acquittal at court. There have been statutes setting the age at from twelve to eighteen in the United States; and the Model Penal Code drafted in 1962 after approximately ten years of study by the American Law Institute settled on the age of ten (Dolgin and Dolgin 1980). Since minors cannot give consent, consent is an irrelevant consideration, and at court penalties for having sex with a person below the age of consent—statutory rape—are among the most severe handed down in any cases of rape.

In the United States there is a diversity of sex laws and penalties for their infringement among the fifty states, but every state has some legislation designed to protect children from sexual activity. Such activity is always given a negative label—such as sexual abuse or statutory rape—and the child, being below the age of consent, is labeled the victim. His or her older partner is labeled the perpetrator. Impairing of the morals of a minor, lewd acts, obscenities, and indecent exposure may be defined as misdemeanors, and abduction of minors for sexual use, carnal abuse, genital contact, and forcible or statutory rape may be defined as felonies.

It is difficult to deal with cases of sexual activity involving children within the judicial system. Since witnesses and corroborating evidence are commonly not available, the prosecutor's case often depends almost solely on the child's testimony. Can a child too young to give consent, supposedly too naive to know what is going on or why it is going on, be sophisticated enough to give testimony? Furthermore, can a child who has seen no other sexual activity, heard of none, and not experienced any but that involved in the case in question be subjected to the rigors of an adversarial proceeding? There is concern about this, and the courts go to great pains to secure the needed evidence while at the same time attempting to minimize psychological trauma suffered by the child during the criminal trial process. Lawyers and judges refer to the "trauma" of the child who must face many strangers in the criminal system, and to the child as a "psychologically sensitive victim" (Oseid 1985:1380). In most jurisdictions in the United States, a trial judge may make a finding of competency when convinced that a child witness can intelligently relate the facts, distinguish between the truth and lies, and understand the importance of an oath or the consequences of lying.

Not all persons subscribe completely to a protection paradigm in dealing with children, though some elements of protection must be a part of any paradigm because of the high level of dependency of human offspring from birth and at least for several years. Socializing is still the major mode of child rearing in the West. A major competing paradigm is the personal paradigm. A number of lists of essential rights of children have been proposed within this personal paradigm. Most of them appeared during the 1970s, the time of an early aborted Children's Liberation Movement in the United States (Farson 1974; Foster and Freed 1972; Gross and Gross 1977; Holt 1974). All proponents of children's rights would grant to children the same rights as are granted to adults, including the right to choose guardians and living arrangements, to exercise political and economic power, and to receive information; and some would grant the right of sexual freedom (Calderone 1977; Farson 1974; Gross and Gross 1977). According to Calderone, the fundamental sexual rights of children would include the right to know about sexuality, the right to be sexual, and the right of access to educational and literary sexual materials. In part, the personal paradigm is based on the belief that the child knows better than the adult what it needs at each stage of its life and that adults, particularly parents, interact with the child in such a way as to empathize with and fulfill the child's particular and expanding needs. Nowhere in the West are child–adult sexual acts generally regarded as a right; the child's right to masturbate and the right of children to engage in sex play and other forms of intimacy with each other is most clearly recognized in certain Scandinavian countries (Aigner and Centerwall 1984).

Legislative trends tend to shift in concert with other social changes, but there is likely to be considerable lag when law and judicial decisions are involved. Both tend to express the specific, concrete concerns and the social policies of a past generation. This is particularly true in regard to child law and judicial decisions, since child law is created and enforced by an adult population and not necessarily a population in tune with or empathetic to the needs and interest of children. Considerations of paternalism are especially strong in child law as adult lawmakers and enforcers attempt to protect what are regarded as weak, innocent, and hence potentially exploitable children.

For example, the state of California has no less than eight different statutory proceedings that can affect the custody of a child. The concept that is supposed to take precedence in awarding custody is the best interest of the child (Child 1982). It is a moot question how much input the child has in assessing his or her best interest, for the custody statute is silent on some important issues and is vague on others. This, along with a collection of inconsistent court opinions for precedents, means that judges may do with their discretion virtually whatever they will. According to Dolgin and address the problem within a broader context. In subsection 5(3) of the Act as amended, the term *sexual abuse* includes "the obscene or pornographic photographing, filming or depiction of children for commercial purposes, or the rape, molestation, incest, prostitution, or other such forms of sexual exploitation of children under circumstances which indicate that the child's health or welfare is harmed or threatened thereby" (*Congressional Record—House*, p. H2647, April 10, 1978). The National Center for Child Abuse and Neglect adopted a tentative definition of child sexual abuse as "contacts or interactions between a child and an adult when the child is being used for the sexual stimulation of the perpetrator or another person. Sexual abuse may also be committed by a person under the age of 18 when that person is either significantly older than the victim or when the perpetrator is in a position of power or control over another child."

Child protection and pornography legislation of 1984 further criminalized sexual activity in which children are involved. Federal laws against the production and distribution of pornographic materials involving children raised the age of consent from sixteen to eighteen, removed an existing requirement that sexually explicit materials depicting children be obscene before they may be banned, and banned the production and distribution of child pornography regardless of whether it was commercially disseminated (HR3635-PL98-292). According to Money (1985:85), "strictly speaking, the law makes it a crime for parents to send their baby's grandparents a nude picture of the baby, genitals exposed in the bathtub."

Through the monitoring of child–adult behavior by other adults, it is possible that some cases of child sexual abuse come to light and are treated. It is also possible that the laws and monitoring deter others from abusive sexual practices. Such outcomes are positive and should be applauded. But because of the vagueness and inclusiveness of the definitions of sexual abuse, there is also some danger that increased monitoring and criminalizing of intimate encounters in which children are involved may also have negative effects. VOCAL (Victims of Child Abuse Laws), for example, is a group of adults who organized in part to counteract the overzealous attempt to expose child sex offenders. The definition of what is appropriate intimacy between an adult and a child can be a moot question given the zealous attempt to improve the situation. As Brant and Tisza (1977) have stated it,

> tender fondling by the parents may transgress strict boundaries; in the twilight state of mutual affection, unconscious wishes and vivid fantasies may emerge, and incest may become an emotional experience for a child even without direct genital contact . . . [I]t is hard to

define the point at which pleasurable stimulation is experienced as over stimulation, and the child, flooded with excitement, feels overwhelmed and helpless, fears loss of control, and becomes symptomatic. It is difficult to ascertain at what point an experience engenders an individual child's reaction of anxiety and guilt. (Brant and Tisza 1977:85)

In sum, some sex involving minors is being decriminalized and some is being criminalized at the present. As U.S. society is doing what it can to protect children from exploitation, it may also limit children's expression of their sexuality through the legal restraints put on parents and other of the child's potential partners in intimacy. Carolyn Swift testified on sexual assault on children and adolescents before a subcommittee of the U.S. House of Representatives. She stated that children are the least articulate and most exploited population "suffering from society's failure to confront realistically the phenomenon of human sexuality" (testimony proposed for the Subcommittee on Science and Technology, January 11, 1978).

Several consequences grow out of society's reluctance to confront realistically the phenomenon of human sexuality: (1) the lack of willingness to fund research on children's sexuality; (2) the unwillingness to inform children about human sexuality, including their own sexuality; (3) the decriminalization of sexual activity, and therefore the exposure of children to exploitation; and (4) the criminalization of other aspects of sexuality, and therefore limitation of the opportunity for erotic and sexual experiences of children.

Despite limited societal interest in finding out the nature of child sexuality and the lack of funding of child sex research, there has been a slow increment in knowledge of child sexuality (Constantine and Martinson 1981; Samson 1980). It is now becoming common in the Western world to grant that children *are* sexual, though they may still be denied full rights to behave sexually. Compared with earlier decades, perhaps most parents today accept that children masturbate and agree that it is all right; many would allow their young children to engage in some peer sex play and exploration; but perhaps most, even advocates of children's rights, might be expected to rule out child–adult sexual activity.

Both conservatives and liberals agree that clear breaches of sexual etiquette that are infringements of basic rights and are physically and psychologically injurious to children, such as rape, should be punished. But otherwise the conservative and liberal views on child sexuality are likely endpoints on a continuum with many shades of difference in between and with the unaligned majority leaning toward either polar position or finding themselves somewhere in between (Scanzoni 1983). There is a large gray area constituting what types of intimacy are appropriate, healthful, and enjoyable for children—the large gray area between tender loving care at one end of the continuum and rape at the other. There is also profound disagreement on the importance of consent, what consent means, who is mature enough to give consent, and whether consent laws (beyond the protection against violation and abuse granted to all citizens) are necessary. In other words, the issue of consent remains remarkably difficult.

Strong support for the conventional sexuality, even the authority system of the patriarchal family, comes from the so-called Christian Right, which is vocally and politically active both in the United States and Europe. Respect for authority is central to the perspective of the Christian Right— the child's respect for the authority of his or her parents, the wife for the husband's authority, and the husband for God's authority. There are eight causes of today's family breakdown according to LaHaye and LaHaye (1978), who speak for the Christian Right, and several of them are particularly hazardous for children and the sexual upbringing of children—the dominance of atheistic, anti-Christian humanism in schools and the media; sexual immorality and promiscuity; legalization of pornography; and a permissive philosophy of child rearing. In the United States, the Christian Right and other elements of the conservative movement have demonstrated substantial political power in crippling sex education programs in the schools.

Turning now to the liberal pole, departures from a conservative stance are not new (Blatz 1944), nor in some ways are they as conspicuous as they were in the short-lived Child Liberation Movement of the 1970s in the United States. It may sound at first blush as though the liberal jurist Brongersma is speaking the same language as the Christian Right when he states that "we fight only for the right to be more human and the right of the young ones to be loved" (Brongersma 1977:4). But the love Brongersma refers to includes erotic and sexual love, and the Christian Right would reject the statement as both humanistic and sexually aberrant.

Liberals draw heavily on recent and current research on the sexual nature of the child and child sexual experiences and generally support children's rights. As Constantine (1983:258) stated, "If they are considered to be sexual beings with the rights to express themselves sexually, then not all sexual contact between adults and children can be categorically depressed as abuse."

In the Netherlands, for example, the National Council for Mental Health, a federation of all mental health agencies, after a two-year study concluded that sections of the penal law directed against sexual activities with a consenting partner, whatever his or her age, should be abolished.

According to Constantine, a rationalized legal framework that recognized the right of the child to a free choice of sexual partners would entail informed consent and participation of the child and would exclude the use of force, coercion, or psychological pressure:

> If the child was not fully knowledgeable of the nature of the sexual activity or was demonstrably not capable of informed consent, or if any force or coercion was employed, sex between an adult and a child would constitute rape of a minor. A statement by a minor that he or she did not feel free to refuse should be a prima facie case for rape. An extra burden would thus appropriately be placed on the physically and intellectually more powerful adult to assure that the participation of the child was both informed and voluntary. (Constantine and Martinson 1981:259)

Will the future bring any notable shifts in perspective on children and children's rights and freedom, including sexual rights and freedom either in the conservative or liberal direction? The conservatives clearly appear to be better organized, more tenacious, and have more political clout than the liberals. On the other hand, programmatic fragmentation characterizes the liberals. According to Scanzoni (1983:197), "progressives have been unable to conjure a vision of family comparable in scope, coherence, and persuasiveness to that of the conservative visions." This is not the situation in some of the Northern European countries, where social democrats have fairly well-articulated perspectives and political programs on the family, on child care, and to some extent even on sexual rights of children.

But the issue goes deeper than vision, persuasion, and organization, of course. Fundamental change in perspective on childhood might well require a reconceptualization of childhood (Gil 1974). Such a radical transformation from protection to personal paradigm with respect to children's rights is unlikely to occur in the West in the foreseeable future. The social systems involved generally subscribe to protective paradigms. Nor will legislators and the courts institute marked change away from child sex law that emphasizes protection of children to child sex law that emphasizes protection of their rights and freedoms, for legislative and legal trends tend to shift in concert with other social alternatives.

From a different perspective, whereas the law is inclined to preserve the past while reflecting current sociocultural consensus, researchers who are committed to social justice for all and who conceive of social science as a tool in the struggle for human liberation conduct studies of alternative social patterns and lifestyles that may challenge prevailing assumptions and that hold promise for human existence freed of potential injustices in the prevailing social order.

Historians of childhood in the Western world have focused on what they regard as marked changes in conceptualization of the child, children's rights, and child rearing—from the lack of a concept of children as a separate entity, great cruelty to children, and obsession with discipline in the sixteenth century, to more human methods of discipline in the mid-eighteenth century (Pollock 1983). Pollock (1983), using over 500 diaries, autobiographies, and manuscripts from the sixteenth to the eighteenth century, concluded that there have only been slight changes in the conception of childhood and great variety in child care patterns in each century.

The link between child-rearing behavior and societal values placed on the child may be more complex than realized. The dependent nature of children and the nature of parenting may be impervious to sociocultural values.

If the first aspect of the child's right to sex freedom is his or her right to information about sexuality, then (as indicated in Chapter 7) there is evidence that children have gained some ground. Studies in the last few years show that a majority of parents want their children to have sexual education. But a program of comprehensive sexual education for all children is too much to expect, given the protective perspective on children prevailing in the United States and in some European countries (Jackson 1982).

REFERENCES

Aigner, G. and E. Centerwall. *Barnas Kjaerlighotsliv*. Oslo: Pax Forlag, 1984.

Blatz, W. *Understanding the Young Child*. Toronto: Clark-Ervin, 1944.

Brant, R.S.T. and V. B. Tisza. "The Sexually Misused Child." *American Journal of Orthopsychiatry* 47(1977):80–90.

Brongersma, E. "Aggression against Pedophiles." *International Journal of Law and Psychiatry* 7(1984):7, 79–87.

Brongersma, E. "On Loving Relationships Human and Humane." *Childhood Rights* 1(1977):1.

Calderone, M. S. "Sexual Rights." *SIECUS Report* 5(1977):3.

Child, B. "The Nonmarital Sexual Conduct of Custodial Mothers: A Study of California's Precarious Parental Rights." *Golden Gate University Law Review* 12(1982):505–36.

Constantine, L. L. "Child Sexuality: Recent Developments and Implications for Treatment, Prevention, and Social Policy." *Medicine and Law* 2(1983):55–67.

Constantine, L. L. "The Sexual Rights of Children: Implications of a Radial Perspective." In *Children and Sex: New Findings, New Perspectives*, edited by L. L. Constantine and F. M. Martinson, 255–63.

Constantine, L. L. and F. M. Martinson. *Children and Sex: New Findings, New Perspectives*. Boston: Little, Brown, 1981.

DeMause, L. "The Evolution of Childhood." *Psychological Abstracts* 1(1974):503–73.

Dolgin, J. L. and B. L. Dolgin. "Sex and the Law." In *Handbook of Human Sexuality*, edited by B. B. Wolman and J. Money, 202–24.

Farson, R. *Birthrights*. New York: Macmillan, 1974.

Foster, H. H. and D. J. Freed. "A Bill of Rights for Children." *Family Law Quarterly* 6(1972):343–75.

Gil, D. G. "A Holistic Perspective on Child Abuse and Its Prevention." *Journal of Sociology and Social Welfare* 2(1974):110–25.

Ginnow, A. O. and G. Gordon. *Corpus Juris Secumdum*. St. Paul: West Publishing Company, 1978.

Gross, B. and R. Gross (eds.). *The Children's Rights Movement*. Garden City: Anchor/Doubleday, 1977.

Holt, J. *Escape from Childhood: The Needs and Rights of Children*. New York: Ballantine, 1974.

Jackson, S. *Childhood and Sexuality*. Oxford: Basil Blackwell, 1982.

Kalvin, H., Jr. and H. Zeisel. *The American Jury*. Boston: Little, Brown, 1966.

LaHaye, T. and B. LaHaye. *Spirit-controlled Family Living*. Old Tappan, N.J.: Fleming H. Revell, 1978.

Lee, J. A. "The Politics of Child Sexuality." In *Childhood and Sexuality*, edited by J.-M. Samson, 56–70. Montreal: Editions Etudes Vivantes, 1980.

Martindale-Hubbel Law Directory VII. Summit, N.J.: Martindale-Hubbel Inc., 1984.

Martinson, F. M. "Current Legal Status of the Erotic and Sexual Rights of Children." In *Handbook of Sexology*, edited by M. E. Perry, 113–24. Amsterdam: Elsevier, 1990.

Money, J. "The Conceptual Neutering of Gender and the Criminalization of Sex." *Archives of Sexual Behavior* 14(1985):279–90.

Oseid, J. "Defendants' Rights in Child Witness Competency Hearings: Establishing Constitutional Procedures for Sexual Abuse Cases." *Minnesota Law Review* 69(1985):1377–99.

Pollock, L. A. *Forgotten Children: Parent-Child Relations from 1500 to 1900*. Cambridge: Cambridge University Press, 1983.

Rachford, B. K. "Pseudomasturbation in Infants." *Archives of Pediatrics* XXIV(1907):561–89.

Rush, F. *The Best Kept Secret: Sexual Abuse of Children*. Englewood Cliffs, N.J: Prentice Hall, 1980.

Samson, J.-M. *Childhood and Sexuality*. Montreal: Editions Etudes Vivantes, 1980.

Scanzoni, J. *Shaping Tomorrow's Family: Theory and Policy for the 21st Century*. Beverly Hills: Sage Publications, 1983.

Sears, R. R., E. E. Maccoby, and H. Levine. *Patterns of Child Rearing*. Evanston, Ill.: Row, Peterson, 1957.

Ullerstam, L. *The Erotic Minorities*. New York: Grove Press, 1966.

9

The Sexual Life of Children: Sweden and the United States

As one expert on sexually victimized children wrote, "we know more about sexual deviance than we do about sexual normality . . . [W]e hardly know how they come to have sexual experience at all." We have "a vast ignorance of the forces governing the development and experience of sexual behavior in general" (Finkelhor 1979:20).

How do children get a sexual life? This is a question that has not been asked seriously. They appear to get it naturally and unobtrusively by being alert to the many influences around them. But that method is not sufficient in a society where pains are taken to keep as much sexuality hidden from children as is possible. In such a society, if we want children to know about sexuality, we need to supplement natural assimilation with instruction.

Goldman and Goldman provided a "natural experiment" on the need for sexual education in their book *Children's Sexual Thinking* (1982). They were two Australian educators looking for the best in sexual education materials and methods. They hit on an ingenious method of determining the value of sexual education programs by interviewing a sample of five- to fifteen-year-olds in four countries—Australia, England, Sweden, and the United States.

Children's sexual thinking is not confined to thinking about sexual intercourse. It embraces a much broader universe of experiences than that, and Goldman and Goldman used the broadest meaning of sexuality in planning an completing their research.

The child is a sexual thinker from birth. Children constantly seek for sex information by whatever ingenious method they can. Their interest in exploring sexual topics increases as their age increases, until they feel that they have a fairly complete set of answers. If they do not get answers, they invent them.

Goldman and Goldman found that children in the United States were receiving the least and the latest sexual education, while in Sweden sexual education was provided to children from the first grade, age seven and on. Here we have our "natural experiment"—one country with the least and the latest sexual education, another country with the earliest sexual education. What differences did Goldman and Goldman find between children in the two countries?

Goldman and Goldman found Swedish children to be capable of understanding complex biological concepts much earlier than had been believed. They were two or more years ahead in sexual knowledge and understanding. In the United States children were retarded in their sexual knowledge three or more years—the most retarded of all four countries. The authors were convinced that the American children were inadequately prepared for sexual adulthood. For example, American children gave nonsexual responses to parent roles in procreation. Such answers were strongly in evidence up to and including eleven years of age. Many older children knew the facts of sexual joining, but few could put the facts together to make a satisfactory explanation, even by age fifteen. (Only an estimated 10 percent of American high school students receive comprehensive sex education before they graduate from high school today.)

At the same time, the home was the most cited major source of sex information for children, in the person of the mother. Could it be that silence in the school is matched by silence in the home as well? I suspect that it is. The Sears, Maccoby, and Levine study done in New England (1957) bears this out. One can only be amazed by the ingenious means mothers utilized to thwart the attempts of their young children to engage in sex play and to ask sex questions. Not one parent was completely free and open in the discussion of sex. One reason why parents were not open was the fear that any attention called to the subject of sex might awaken the child to erotic activity. Parents in the Berges study (1991) never brought up the subject of orgasm with their children. They did not believe that their children had any understanding of what orgasm was. Nor is orgasm a topic commonly discussed in books on sex education prepared for parents of children in U.S. society (Martinson 1992).

Beginning in the 1800s, U.S. society built a wall around children to protect their innocence and to protect them from their own sexual inclinations. Keeping children sexually innocent became firmly established and has continued to be a feature of American culture. This means that teenagers have to look elsewhere for their final sexual instruction. Their peers are a major source. They learn from their peers what passion is. They learn the joy, the fear, the excitement in sexuality. They learn about orgasm. They learn the status that sexuality can bring.

Engaging in premarital sexual intercourse has become statistically normative for American youth. Fifty-four percent of ninth through twelfth graders and 72 percent of high school seniors have had sexual intercourse (Haffner 1992). An estimated 30 percent of sexually active adolescents become pregnant. Even among those girls in the lowest age categories (fifteen to seventeen), 4 percent have had more than ten different partners. Sexually transmitted diseases—gonorrhea, chlamydia, herpes, and cervical cancer—are occurring at high levels in the United States, and adolescents are both the recipients and the transmitters of these infections (Fisher 1990).

Sweden took another course. It introduced sex education in 1942 and made it compulsory in 1956. After studying its program in the late 1970s, Sweden reduced the age at which each topic was offered. Between the ages of seven and ten, Swedish pupils learned the difference between the sexes, where babies come from, the father's role in conception, developments before birth, the process of birth, and many other topics. The Swedes were still not satisfied with their program and introduced a more difficult subject of sex education—namely, teaching children the art of loving. They reason that sexuality is not a bad habit to be discarded. Sex education is important for a happy life. Sex is not a secret in Sweden. Sex education is a totally open program based on faith in young people. And the young people have responded. They understand about sexuality at an early age. The rate of sexual intercourse is not down (Schwartz 1993), but the rates of venereal disease and abortion are. Sweden's abortion rates are lower than the latest figures for Australia, the United States, and England and Wales (Goldman and Goldman 1982).

I do not know what the outcome of the American program will be. Premarital sexual intercourse is a moral issue for some adults, and this is part of the problem. Sexual education has focused, grudgingly I would say, on helping young people avoid the negative consequences of bad decisions that could lead to contracting sexually transmitted diseases, unplanned and unwanted pregnancies, school dropouts, early marriage, and a life of poverty. However, there is a new view, almost in the spirit of the Swedes, that sees sexuality as a matter of health, not illness, and tries to help people accept and enjoy their overall mental and social health and well-being. It is argued that a major source of public schooling should be to teach children how to reason, to question, and to accept responsibility—to teach them *how* to think, more than *what* to think. Public education has an obligation to present a variety of ideas that reflect the perspectives of the entire community and to address the needs of all pupils, starting in kindergarten (Sedway 1992). They have introduced a K–12 curriculum. On the other side, there are groups (often referred to as the far right or religious right) who promote a narrower curriculum that eliminates the discussion of controversial topics (such as birth control, AIDS, and abortion) and focuses almost exclusively on sexual abstinence as the only behavior that can be supported for moral or practical reasons. These groups also are introducing curricula, and they are small but fervent and zealous. We can say as Udry (1993:109) did about sex research that it "is not a battle between the forces of good and evil . . . nor is it a battle based on some misunderstanding that can be made to go away by more communication. On the contrary. It is a genuine and legitimate political battle between two groups and the population who hold diametrically opposed policy views." It is too soon to say which side will win.

For nearly twenty-five years now, the attention of scholars in America (and, incidentally, most of the research money) has been concentrated on a much smaller but not inconsequential problem: child sexual abuse. I cannot help but feel that the problem is exacerbated by our concern over the naiveté of our youth, caught up as they are in a much larger political and religious issue—an issue not of their making. They are being blamed for sexual issues that are not of their making, either. For example, we use the perspective of victimology in judging sexual cases. Victimization predicates victims and perpetrators. The perpetrator is a human being who must be segregated from society or otherwise disciplined. We have begun to use this paradigm in dealing with child sexuality and have written it into the law. Behavior that I found was still treated as child sex play in Scandinavia, at least up until 1984 (Aigner and Centerwall 1984), was treated as perpetrator-victim behavior in the United States.

The following are examples of the effect of the use of the victim and perpetrator paradigm in dealing with children. The state of Minnesota reported 1,110 cases of sexual harassment and ninety-five cases of sexual violence in its schools in 1991–92, and they were only the cases that were reported (Hotakainen 1993). It is alleged that many more were not reported. More than 1,000 children in the city of Minneapolis alone were suspended or expelled on charges of sexual harassment (Shalit 1993). Cases such as the following were classified as sexual harassment: telling dirty jokes, spreading rumors about sexual behavior of individual girls, exposing oneself, snapping bras, wearing offensive T-shirts, and yelling sexual innuendoes during sporting events. Cases classified as sexual violence, the more serious cases, included rape, forced fondling and touching, forced oral sex, "depantsing" (removing another's pants as a joke or as punishment), and "sharking" (biting body parts, such as breasts).

Punishment for such offenses, besides expulsion, included transfer to another school, writing essays, apologizing, undergoing counseling, and serving time in detention. The attorney general of the state of Minnesota has warned Minnesota children that such behavior can result in costly litigation. Minnesota is viewed as a national leader in fighting sexual harassment.

Sue Sattel, a specialist for the Minnesota Department of Education, reported what she regarded as an open-and-shut case of sexual harassment involving a five-year-old boy as predator and a five-year-old girl as victim. She reported, "The boy led the girl into the art resource room. He pulled her pants down. He pulled his own pants down. He jumped on top of her. And he began simulated sexual intercourse." Sattel said, "Something very, very serious is going to happen to that little boy" (Shalit 1993:13). And she is right, for this is a sexual offense in most states. Minnesota's anti-sexual-harassment law covers all children down to and including the kindergarten age.

A publication provided by the Minnesota Department of Education, *Examples of Hostile Environmental Sexual Harassment*, provides a glimpse into what supervisors are looking for on the playground. Here is a partial listing:

- Sexual gestures (e.g., boys grabbing their groin when a girl passes by)
- Students "rating" other students
- Students teasing other students about body development, either overdevelopment or underdevelopment
- Males bragging about or indicating the size of their penis

Proponents of Minnesota law say tough penalties for offenses like these are the wave of the future.

As I said at the beginning of this chapter, children appear to get a sexual life naturally and unobtrusively by being alert to the many influences around them. But are these the influences that children are being alerted to? They come at an age when children are concerned about their own identity and how to relate to members of the other sex. And in their fumbling attempts to relate, they often perform badly. It is a moot question whether such behavior should be handled punitively, with more expulsion and more detention and at younger ages, or whether we should try another perspective, such as teaching the art of loving and the respect for others.

REFERENCES

Aigner, G. and E. Centerwall. *Barnas Kjaerlighetsliv*. Oslo: Pax Forlag, 1984.

Berges, E. T., S. Neiderbach, B. Rubin, E. F. Sharpe, and R. W. Tesler. *Children and Sex: The Parents Speak*. New York: Facts on File, 1983.

Finkelhor, D. *Sexually Victimized Children*. New York: Free Press, 1979.

Fisher, W. A. "An Integrated Approach to Preventing Adolescent Pregnancy and STD/HIV Infection." *SIECUS Report* 18(1990):1–11.

Goldman R. and J. Goldman. *Children's Sexual Thinking*. London: Routledge and Kegan Paul, 1982.

Haffner, D. "Youth Still at Risk, Yet Barriers to Sex Education Remain." *SIECUS Report* 21(1992):10–12.

Hotakainen, R. "School Quizzed on Sexual Harassment." *Star Tribune* April 30, 1993, 1B and 4B.

Johnson, T. "Child Sexual Perpetrator—Children Who Molest Other Children: Preliminary Findings." *Child Abuse and Neglect* 12(1988):219–29.

Johnson, T. "Female Child Perpetrators: Children Who Molest Other Children." *Child Abuse and Neglect* 13(1989):571–85.

Martinson, F. M. "Child Sexual Development and Experience: What the Experts Are Telling Parents." Paper presented at The Society for the Scientific Study of Sex annual meeting, November 1992.

Money, J. "Sexology and/or Sexosophy." *SIECUS Report* 19(1989):1–4.

Schwartz, F. M. "Affective Reactions of American and Swedish Women to Their First Premarital Coitus: A Cross-Cultural Comparison." 30(1993):18–26.

Sears, R. R., E. E. Maccoby, and H. Levine. *Patterns of Child Rearing*. Evanston, Ill.: Row, Peterson, 1957.

Sedway, M. "The Right Takes Aim at Sexuality Education." *SIECUS Report* 20(1992):13–19.

Shalit, R. "Romper Room." *The New Republic* March 29, 1993, 13–15.

Udry, J. R. "The Politics of Sex Research." *Journal of Sex Research* 30(1993):103–10.

Bibliography

Abel, G., M. Mittelman, and J. Becker. "Sexual Offenders: Results of Assessment and Recommendation of Treatment." In *Clinical Criminology: The Assessment and Treatment of Criminal Behavior*, edited by M. H. Ben-Aron, S. J. Hacker, and E. D. Webster. Toronto: Butterworth, 1987.

Abramovitch, R., D. Pepler, and C. Corter. "Patterns of Sibling Interaction Among Preschool-age Children." In *Sibling Relations*, edited by M. E. Lamb and B. Sutton-Smith, 61–86. Hillsdale, N.J.: Lawrence Erlbaum Associates, 1982.

Aigner, G., and E. Centerwall. *Barnas Kjaerlighetsliv*. Oslo: Pax Forlag, 1984.

Ainsworth, M. D. "Patterns of Attachment Behavior Shown by the Infant in Interaction with His Mother." *Merrill-Palmer Quarterly* 10(1964):51–58.

Alexander, P. "A Systems Theory Conceptualization of Incest." *Family Process* 24(1985):70–88.

Ames, L. B. "Children's Stories." *Genetic Psychology Monographs* 73(1966):337–96.

Baker, E. F. "A Further Study of Genital Anxiety in Nursing Mothers." *The Journal of Orgonomy* 3(1969):46–55.

Barthalow-Koch, P. "A Comparison of the Sex Education of Primary-aged Children in the United States and Sweden as Expressed through Their Art." In *Childhood and Sexuality*, edited by J.-M. Samson, 345–55. Montreal: Editions Etudes Vivantes, 1980.

Bell, S. "A Preliminary Study of the Emotion of Love between the Sexes." *American Journal of Psychology* XIII(1902):325–54.

Berges, E. T., S. Neiderbach, B. Rubin, E. F. Sharpe, and R. W. Tesler. *Children and Sex: The Parents Speak*. New York: Facts on File, 1983.

Bernstein, A. C. and P. A. Cowan. "Children's Concepts of How People Get Babies." *Child Development* 46(1975):77–91.
Blackman, M. "Pleasure and Touching: Their Significance in the Development of the Preschool Child—An Exploratory Study." In *Childhood and Sexuality: Proceedings of the International Symposium*, edited by J.-M. Samson, 175–202. Montreal: Editions Etudes Vivantes, 1980.
Blatz, W. *Understanding the Young Child*. Toronto: Clark-Ervin, 1944.
Borneman, E. "Progress in Empirical Research on Children's Sexuality." *SIECUS Report* 12(1983):1–6.
Bowlby, J. *Child Care and the Growth of Love*, 2nd ed. London: Penguin, 1965.
Brant, R.S.T. and V. B. Tisza. "The Sexually Misused Child." *American Journal of Orthopsychiatry* 47(1977):80–90.
Brick, P. "Sexual Education in the Elementary School." *SIECUS Report* XIII(1985):1–4.
Brill, A. A. *Lectures on Psychoanalytic Psychiatry*. London: J. Lehmann, 1948.
Britten, P. O., D. de Mauro, and A. E. Gambrell. "HIV/AIDS Education." *SIECUS Report* 21(1992):1–8.
Bronfenbrenner, U. *The Ecology of Human Development*. Cambridge, Mass.: Harvard, 1979.
Brongersma, E. "Aggression against Pedophiles." *International Journal of Law and Psychiatry* 7(1984):7, 79.
Brongersma, E. "On Loving Relationships Human and Humane." *Childhood Rights* 1(1977):1.
Burgess, A. W. (ed.). *Child Pornography and Sex Rings*. Lexington, Mass.: Lexington Books, 1984.
Calderone, M. S. "Sexual Rights." *SIECUS Report* 5(1977):3.
Capes, M. "Sexual Development in Childhood and Its Problems." *British Medical Journal* 4(1972):38–39.
Carter-Jessup, L. "Promoting Maternal Attachment through Prenatal Intervention." *Maternal Child Nursing* 6(1981):107–12.
Cassel, Z. K. and L. W. Sander. "Neonatal Recognition Processes and Attachment: The Masking Experiment." Presented at the Society for Research in Child Development, Denver, 1975.
Chasnoff, I. J., W. J. Burns, S. H. Schnoll, K. Burns, G. Chisum, and L. Kyle-Spore. "Maternal-Neonatal Incest." *American Journal of Orthopsychiatry* 56(1986):577–80.
Child, B. "The Nonmarital Sexual Conduct of Custodial Mothers: A Study of California's Precarious Parental Rights." *Golden Gate University Law Review* 12(1982):505–36.
Clark-Stewart, K. A. "Interaction between Others and Their Young Children: Characteristics and Consequences." *Monographs of the Society for Research in Child Development* 38(1973):1–108.

Condon, W. S. and L. W. Sander. "Neonate Movement Is Synchronized with Adult Speech: Interactional Participation and Language Acquisition." *Science* 183(1974):99–101.

Conn. J. H. and L. Kanner. "Children's Awareness of Sex Differences." *Journal of Child Psychiatry* 1(1947):3–57.

Conn, J. H. and L. Kanner. "Spontaneous Erections in Early Childhood." *Journal of Pediatrics* 16(1940):337–40.

Constantine, L. L. "The Effects of Early Sexual Experiences: A Review and Synthesis of Research." In *Children and Sex: New Findings New Perspectives*, edited by L. L. Constantine and F. M. Martinson, 217–44. Boston: Little, Brown, 1981.

Constantine, L. L. "Child Sexuality: Recent Developments and Implications for Treatment, Prevention, and Social Policy." *Medicine and Law* 2(1983):55-67.

Constantine, L. L. "The Sexual Rights of Children: Implications of a Radical Perspective." In *Children and Sex: New Findings, New Perspectives*, edited by L. L. Constantine and F. M. Martinson, 255. Boston: Little, Brown, 1981c.

Constantine, L. L. and F. M. Martinson. *Children and Sex: New Findings, New Perspectives*. Boston: Little, Brown, 1981.

Croft, C. A. and L. Asmussen. "Perceptions of Mothers, Youth, and Educators: A Path Toward Détente Regarding Sexuality Education." *Family Relations* 41(1992):452–59.

Davis, Katherine B. *Factors in the Sex Life of Twenty-Two Hundred Women*. New York: Harper and Bros., 1929.

DeMause, L. "The Evolution of Childhood." *Psychological Abstracts* 1(1974):503–75.

Dolgin, J. L. and B. L. Dolgin. "Sex and the Law." In *Handbook of Human Sexuality*, edited by B. B. Wolman and J. Money, 202. Englewood Cliffs, N.J.: Prentice Hall, 1980.

Dunn, J. B. and M.P.M. Richards. "Observations on the Developing Relationship between Mother and Baby in the Neonatal Period." In *Studies in Mother–Infant Interaction*, edited by H. R. Schaffer, 427–55. London: Academic Press, 1977.

Elias, N. *The History of Manners*. New York: Pantheon, 1978. (Originally published in Switzerland in 1939.)

Ennew, J. *The Sexual Exploitation of Children*. New York: St. Martin's, 1986.

Entwisle, D. R., S. G. Doering, and T. W. Reilly. "Sociopsychological Determinants of Women's Breast-Feeding Behavior: A Replication and Extension." *American Journal of Orthopsychiatry* 52(1982):244–60.

Farson, R. *Birthrights*. New York: Macmillan, 1974.

Field, T. N. "Discrimination and Imitation of Facial Expressions by Neonates." *Science* 218(1982):179–81.

Finkelhor, D. *Sexually Victimized Children*. New York: Free Press, 1979.

Finkelhor, D. "Social Forces in the Formulation of the Problem of Sexual Abuse." *University of New Hampshire Family Violence Research Program*, 5(1978):1–21.

Finkelhor, D. and S. Araji. "Explanations of Pedophilia: A Four Factor Model." *Journal of Sex Research* 22(1986):145–61.

Fisher, W. A. "An Integrated Approach to Preventing Adolescent Pregnancy and STD/HIV Infection." *SIECUS Report* 18(1990):1–11.

Ford, C. S. and F. A. Beach. *Patterns of Sexual Behavior*. New York: Harper, 1951.

Foster, H. H. and D. J. Freed. "A Bill of Rights for Children." *Family Law Quarterly* 6(1972):343–75.

Fraiberg, S. "How a Baby Learns to Love." *Redbook* May 1971.

Freud, S. *The Basic Writings of Sigmund Freud*. New York: Modern Library, 1938. (Translated and edited by A. A. Brill.)

Frude, N. "The Sexual Nature of Sexual Abuse: A Review of the Literature." *Child Abuse and Neglect* 6(1982):211–23.

Gagnon, J. "Female Child Victims of Sex Offenders." *Social Problems* 13(1965):176–92.

Gagnon, J. H. "Attitudes and Responses of Parents to Pre-Adolescent Masturbation." *Archives of Sexual Behavior* 14(1985):451–66.

Gagnon, J H. "Sexuality and Sexual Learning in the Child." *Psychiatry* 28(1965):212–28.

Galenson, E. and H. Roiphe. "The Emergence of Genital Awareness during the Second Year of Life." In *Sex Differences in Behavior*, edited by R. C. Friedman, 233–31. New York: Wiley, 1974.

Gardner, R. A. "Sexual Fantasies in Childhood." *Medical Aspects of Human Sexuality* 3(1969):121, 125, 127–28, 132–34.

Gelles, R. J. and M. A. Straus. *Intimate Violence: The Definitive Study of the Causes and Consequences of Abuse in the American Family*. New York: Simon & Schuster, 1988.

Gil, D. G. "A Holistic Perspective on Child Abuse and Its Prevention." *Journal of Sociology and Social Welfare* 2(1974):110–25.

Gilbert, N. "The Phantom Epidemic of Sexual Assault." *The Public Interest* 103(1991):54–65.

Ginnow, A. O. and G. Gordon. *Corpus Juris Secumdum*. St. Paul: West Publishing Company, 1978.

Giovacchini, P. L. "Promiscuity in Adolescents and Young Adults." *Medical Aspects of Human Sexuality* 20(1986):24–31.

Goldman, R. and J. Goldman. *Children's Sexual Thinking*. London: Routledge and Kegan Paul, 1982.

Goldman, R. and J. Goldman. *Show Me Yours! Understanding Children's Sexuality*. Victoria, Australia: Penguin, 1988.

Goodman, E. "The Risk in Making Sex a Fearsome Thing." *Star Tribune* (Minneapolis), April 4, 1992, 14A.

Gross, B. and R. Gross (eds.). *The Children's Rights Movement*. Garden City: Anchor/Doubleday, 1977.

Groth, A., R. Lango, and J. McFadin. "Undetected Recidivism among Rapists and Child Molesters." *Crime and Delinquency* 28:450–58.

Gundersen, B. H., P. S. Melås, and J. E. Skår. "Sexual Behavior of Preschool Children: Teachers' Observations." In *Children and Sex: New Findings, New Perspectives*, edited by L. L. Constantine and F. M. Martinson, 45–61. Boston: Little, Brown, 1981.

Guyon, R. *The Ethics of Sexual Acts*. New York: Knopf, 1934. (Translated from the French by J. C. and I. Flugel.)

Hacker, S. S. "The Transition from the Old Norm to the New: Sexual Values for the 1990s." *SIECUS Report* 18(1990):1–8.

Haffner, D. "Youth Still at Risk, Yet Barriers to Sex Education Remain." *SIECUS Report* 21(1992):10–12.

Halverson, H. M. "Infant Sucking and Tensional Behavior." *Journal of Genetic Psychology* 32(1938):365–430.

Haugaard, J. J. and N. D. Reppucci. *The Sexual Abuse of Children*. San Francisco: Jossey-Bass, 1988.

Holt, J. *Escape from Childhood: The Needs and Rights of Children*. New York: Ballantine, 1974.

Hopfensperger, Jean. "Looking for Someone to Love: Ranks of Under-15 Mothers Growing" *Star Tribune* July 6, 1993, 1A, 9A.

Hotakainen, R. "School Quizzed on Sexual Harassment." *Star Tribune* April 30, 1993, 1B and 4B.

Hunter, M. *Abused Boys: The Neglected Victims of Sexual Abuse*. Lexington, Mass.: D. C. Heath, 1990.

Jackson, S. *Childhood and Sexuality*. Oxford: Basil Blackwell, 1982.

Johnson, T. "Female Child Perpetrators: Children Who Molest Other Children." *Child Abuse and Neglect* 13(1989):571–85.

Johnson, T. C. "Child Sexual Perpetrator—Children Who Molest Other Children: Preliminary Findings." *Child Abuse and Neglect* 12(1988):219–29.

Johnson, T. C. "Understanding the Sexual Behaviors of Young Children." *SIECUS Report* 19(1991):12–15.

Johnston, C. and R. W. Deisher. "Contemporary Communal Child Rearing: A First Analysis." *Pediatrics* 52(1973):319–26.

Kalvin, H. and H. Zeisel. *The American Jury*. Boston: Little, Brown, 1966.

Kanner, L. "Infantile Sexuality." *Journal of Pediatrics* 4(1939):583–608.

Kaplan, H. S. *the New Sex Therapy*. New York: Brunner/Mazel, 1974.

Kempe, C. H. and others. "The Battered-Child Syndrome." *Journal of the American Medical Association* 181(1962):17–24.

Kilpatrick, A. C. *Long-Range Effects of Child and Adolescent Sexual Experiences*. Hillsdale, N.J.: Lawrence Erlbaum Associates, 1992.

Kinsey, A. C., W. B. Pomeroy, and C. E. Martin. *Sexual Behavior in the Human Male*. Philadelphia: W. B. Saunders, 1948.

Kinsey, A. C., W. B. Pomeroy, C. E. Martin, and P. H. Gebhard. *Sexual Behavior in the Human Female*. Philadelphia: W. B. Saunders, 1953.

Klaus, H. M. and J. H. Kennell. *Maternal-Infant Bonding*. St. Louis: C. V. Mosby, 1976.

Konker, C. "Rethinking Child Sexual Abuse: An Anthropological Perspective." *American Journal of Orthopsychiatry* 62(1992):147–53.

Krueger, M. M. "The Omnipresent Need: Professional Training for Sexuality Education Teachers." *SIECUS Report* 19(1991):1–4.

Kuhn, T. *The Structure of Scientific Revolutions*. Chicago: University of Chicago Press, 1962.

LaHaye, T. and B. LaHaye. *Spirit-controlled Family Living*. Old Tappan, N. J.: Fleming H. Revell, 1978.

Langfeldt, T. "Early Childhood and Juvenile Sexuality, Development and Problems." In *Handbook of Sexuality VII: Childhood and Adolescent Sexology*, edited by M. E. Perry, 179–200. Amsterdam: Elsevier, 1990.

Lee, J. A. "The Politics of Child Sexuality." In *Childhood and Sexuality*, edited by J.-M. Samson, 56. Montreal: Editions Etudes Vivantes, 1980.

Lennard, H. L. and A. Bernstein. *Patterns in Human Interaction*. San Francisco: Jossey-Bass, 1969.

Levine, M. I. "Pediatric Observations on Masturbation in Children." *Psychoanalytic Study of the Child* 6(1957):117–24.

Lewis, W. C. "Coital Movements in the First Year of Life: Earliest Anlage of Genital Love?" *International Journal of Psychoanalysis* 46(1965):372–74.

Lowry, T. P. "How Breast Feeding Arouses Women." *Journal of Sexology* 37(1970):46–49.

Martindale-Hubbel Law Directory VII. Summit, N.J. Martindale-Hubbel Inc., 1984.

Martinson, F. M. "Child Sexual Development and Experience: What the Experts Are Telling Parents." Paper presented at the Society for the Scientific Study of Sex annual meeting, November 1992.

Martinson, F. M. "Current Legal Status of the Erotic and Sexual Rights of Children." In *Handbook of Sexology*, edited by M. E. Perry, 113–24. Amsterdam: Elsevier, 1990.

Masters, W. H. and V. E. Johnson. *Human Sexual Inadequacy*. New York: Little, Brown, 1970.

Masters, W. H. and V. E. Johnson. *Human Sexual Response*. Boston: Little, Brown, 1966.

Miller, A. *Thou Shalt Not Be Aware: Society's Betrayal of the Child*. New York: Farrar, Straus, Giroux, 1984. (Originally published in German 1981.)

Mohr, J. W. "Age Structures in Pedophilia." In *Adult Sexual Interest in Children*, edited by M. Cooke and K. Howells, 41–54. London: Academic, 1981.

Money, J. "The Conceptual Neutering of Gender and the Criminalization of Sex." *Archives of Sexual Behavior* 14(1985):279–90.

Money, J. "Sexology and/or Sexosophy." *SIECUS Report* 19(1989):1–4.
National Guidelines Task Force. *Guidelines for Comprehensive Sexuality Education: Kindergarten–12th Grade.* Sex Information and Education Council of the U.S., 1991.
Nelson, J. "A View Toward Normal, Healthy Incest." *CSC Nusletter* V(1979):4–6.
Newson, J. "An Intersubjective Approach to the Systematic Description of Mother–Infant Interaction." In *Studies in Mother–Infant Interaction*, edited by H. R. Shaffer, 47–61. London: Academic Press, 1977.
Newton, N. "The Role of Oxytocin Reflexes in Three Interpersonal Reproductive Acts: Coitus, Birth and Breastfeeding." *Clinical Psychoneurochronology in Reproduction, Proceedings of the Serono Symposia* 22(1978):411–17.
Newton, N. and M. Newton. "Psychologic Aspects of Lactation." *New England Journal of Medicine* 272(1967):1179–967.
Oseid, J. "Defendants' Rights in Child Witness Competency Hearings: Establishing Constitutional Procedures for Sexual Abuse Cases." *Minnesota Law Review* 69(1985):1377–79.
Parsons, T. "The Incest Taboo in Relation to Social Structure and the Socialization of the Child." *British Journal of Sociology* 5(1954):101–17.
Peters, S. D., G. E. Wyatt, and D. Finkelhor. "Prevalence." In *A Source Book on Sexual Child Abuse*, edited by D. Finkelhor, 75–93. Beverly Hills, CA: Sage, 1986.
Pierce, R. L. "Child Pornography: A Hidden Dimension of Child Abuse." *Child Abuse and Neglect* 8(1984):483–93.
Pitcher, E. G. and E. Prelinger. *Children Tell Stories: An Analysis of Fantasy.* New York: International Universities,1963.
Pollock, L. A. *Forgotten Children: Parent–Child Relations from 1500 to 1900.* Cambridge: Cambridge University Press, 1983.
Rachford, B. K. "Pseudomasturbation in Infants." *Archives of Pediatrics* XXIV(1907):561–89.
Rainwater, L. *Behind Ghetto Walls: Black Families in a Federal Slum.* Chicago: Aldine, 1970.
Ramsey, G. V. "The Sexual Development of Boys." *American Journal of Psychology* 56(1943):217–33.
Reinisch, J. "The Kinsey Report." *Minneapolis Star and Tribune* January 29, 1987, 15D.
Renshaw, D. C. *Sexuality Today* 1(1977):4.
Rice, R. P. "Premature Infants Respond to Sensory Stimulation." *APA Monitor.* As reprinted in *Readings in Human Development*, 1976/1977 annual editions, 60–62, 1975.
Richard, J. "Child Sexuality." *RT-A Journal of Radical Therapy* (1976):1–2.
Roberts, E. J., D. Kline, and J. Gagnon. *Family Life and Sexual Learning, A Study of the Rule of Parents in the Sexual Learning of Children.* Cambridge, Mass.: Population Education Inc., 1978.

Roiphe, H. and E. Galenson. *Infantile Origins of Sexual Identity.* New York: International Universities, 1981.
Rorty, A. O. "Some Social Uses of the Forbidden." *Psychoanalytic Review* 58(1972):497–510.
Rosenfeld, A. A. "Endogamic Incest and the Victim-perpetrator Model." *American Journal of Diseases of Children* 133(1979):406–10.
Rosenfeld, E. L., R. Huesmann, L. D. Eron, and J. V. Torney-Purta. "Measuring Patterns of Fantasy Behavior in Children." *Journal of Personality and Social Psychology* 42(1982):347–66.
Rosenthal, M. K. "Vocal Dialogues in the Neonatal Period." *Developmental Psychology* 18(1982):17–21.
Rush, F. *The Best Kept Secret: Sexual Abuse of Children.* Englewood Cliffs, N.J.: Prentice Hall, 1980.
Samson, J.-M. *Childhood and Sexuality.* Montreal: Editions Etudes Vivantes, 1980.
Sandfort, T. *The Sexual Aspect of Pedophile Relations.* Amsterdam: Pan/Spartacus, 1982.
Sandfort, T.G.M. and W.T.A. Everaerd. "Male Juvenile Partners in Pedophilia." In *Handbook of Sexology VII Childhood and Adolescent Sexuality,* edited by M. E. Perry, 261–80. Amsterdam: Elsevier, 1990.
Scales, P. "Barriers to Sex Education." *Journal of School Health* 50(1980):337–42.
Scales, P. "The Changing Context of Sexual Education: Paradigms and Challenges for Alternative Futures." *Family Relations* 35(1986):265–74.
Scanzoni, J. *Shaping Tomorrow's Family: Theory and Policy for the 21st Century.* Beverly Hills: Sage Publications, 1983.
Schaefer, Leah C. *Sexual Experiences and Reactions of a Group of Thirty Women as Told to a Female Psychotherapist.* Report of an Ed.D. doctoral project. Columbia University, 1964.
Schwartz, F. M. "Affective Reactions of American and Swedish Women to Their First Premarital Coitus: A Cross-Cultural Comparison." *Journal of Sex Research* 30(1993):18–26.
Sears, R. R., E. E. Maccoby, and H. Levine. *Patterns of Child Rearing.* Evanston, Ill.: Row, Peterson, 1957.
Sedway, M. "The Right Takes Aim at Sexuality Education." *SIECUS Report* 20(1992):13–19.
Shalit, R. "Romper Room." *The New Republic* March 29, 1993, 13–15.
Silverstein, C. D. and G. M. Buck. "Parental Preferences Regarding Sex Education Topics for 6th Graders." *Adolescence* XXI(1986):971–80.
Spiro, M. E. *Children of the Kevutza.* Cambridge, Mass.: Harvard University, 1958.
Spitz, R. A. "Autoerotism: Some Empirical Findings and Hypothesis on Three of Its Manifestations in the First Year of Life." *The Psychoanalytic Study of the Child* III/IV(1949):85–120.

Spitz, R. A. and K. W. Wolf. "Anaclitic Depression." *Psychoanalytic Study of the Child* 2(1946):313–42.

Sroufe, L. A. and M. J. Ward. "Seductive Behavior of Mothers of Toddlers: Occurrence, Correlates, and Family Origins." *Child Development* 51(1980):1222–229.

Summit, R. and J. Kryso. "Sexual Abuse of Children: A Clinical Spectrum." *American Journal of Orthopsychiatry* 48(1978):237–51.

Thorne, B. "Girls and Boys Together . . . But Mostly Apart: Gender Arrangements in Elementary Schools." In *Relationships and Development*, edited by W. W. Hartup and Z. Rubin, 161–84. Hillsdale, N.J.: Lawrence Erlbaum Associates, 1985.

Thorne, B. and Z. Luria. "Sexuality and Gender in Children's Daily Worlds." *Social Problems* 33(1986):176–80.

Tsukada, G. K. "Sibling Interaction: A Review of the Literature." *Smith College Studies in Social Work* 49(1979):229–47.

Ullerstam, L. *The Erotic Minorities*. New York: Grove Press, 1966.

Wermer, H. and S. Levin. "Masturbation Fantasies: Their Changes with Growth and Development." *The Psychoanalytic Study of the Child* XXII(1967):315–28.

Udry, J. R. "The Politics of Sex Research." *Journal of Sex Research* 30(1993):103–110.

Wrage, K. *Man and Woman: The Basics of Sex and Marriage*. Philadelphia: Fortress, 1969. (Originally published in German in 1966.)

Yates, A. "Children Eroticized by Incest." *American Journal of Psychiatry* 139(1982):482–85.

Yates, A. "Eroticized Children." In *Handbook of Sexology VII: Childhood and Adolescent Sexology*, edited by M. E. Perry, 325–34. Amsterdam: Elsevier, 1990.

Yates, A. *Sex without Shame: Encouraging the Child's Healthy Sexual Development*. New York: William Morrow, 1978.

Index

Abel, G., 95
Abramovitch, R. D., 92
abuse. *See* child sexual abuse
adolescence, 41, 55n
Africa, 53, 82
age-variant sexual activity: abuse factor and, 86–89; accidental nature of, 75; age differences and, 75, 79–80; anal intercourse and, 82–83; ancient Rome and, 120; cultural acceptance of, 82, 83–84; effects of, 97; exhibition and, 75–78; fellatio and, 82; older acquaintances and, 80; parent-child relationship and, 90–91; pedophilia and, 93–95; physical contact and, 78–80; prevalence of, 75; prostitution and, 96–97; research on, 86; sex rings and, 95–96; sexual knowledge and, 80–82, 85–86; sibling relationships and, 91–93
AIDS education, 113–14
The American Jury, 124
American Law Institute, 122
Ames, L. B., 67, 68
Araji, S., 94
Arapaho, 84
Asmussen, L., 109

Australia, 84, 87, 117
Austria, 45, 69
autoerotism. *See* self-stimulation

Beach, F. A., 57
Becker, J., 95
Behind Ghetto Walls, 102
Bell, S., 36
Berges, E. T., 32, 62, 134
Borneman, E., 45, 69
Bowlby, J., 91
Brant, R.S.T., 95, 126–27
breast-feeding, 8–10
Britain, 30, 117, 122, 124
British Guiana, 84
Brongersma, E., 121, 125, 128
Burgess, A. W., 95, 96

Calderone, M. S., 123
California, 123
Capes, M., 30
Carolines, 84
The Center for Family Life Education, 113
Cheyenne, 84
Child Abuse Prevention and Treatment Act, 125–26

child liberation, 16
Children's Liberation Movement, 123, 128
Children's Sexual Thinking, 133
child sensuality, 1–2, 4–5
Child Sensuality Circle, 16
child (sex) laws: abuse definition and, 125–27; age of minority and, 121–22; ancient Rome and, 120; changes in, 121; child's sexuality and, 127; conceptual changes and, 125, 129–30; consent issue and, 124, 128, 129; conservative *v.* liberal perspectives and, 128–29; custody and, 123; diversity of, 122; functional incest and, 124–25; judiciary and, 122, 123–24; pedophilia and, 125; personal paradigm and, 120, 123, 125, 128–29; pornography and, 126; property paradigm and, 120; protection paradigm and, 120–23, 125–27, 129; sexual harassment and, 137; social changes and, 123; statutory rape and, 124; variable competence and, 124; victims of, 126–27
child sexual abuse: age-variant sex studies and, 86; child sex laws and, 125; defining, 87–89, 125–26; infant orgasms and, 23; overeroticization and, 15; pedophilia and, 94, 95; sexuality education and, 136; violence and, 95
child sexuality: activity percentages and, 87; breast-feeding and, 9–10; cultural differences and, 83–84; dreams and, 67, 68, 70; economic status and, 102; eroticization process and, 11; family interaction and, 15–16, 89–92; fetal stage and, 2; ignorance of, 133; infant care and, 11; infant orgasms and, 23; infant pelvic thrusts and, 7–8; lack of eroticism and, 13–14, 17; myths and, 72–73; orgasmic ability and, 23; overeroticization and, 14–16; parental intimacy and, 12–13; positive *v.* negative feelings toward, 86–87; recognition of, 127; remembrance of experience and, 24; sexual knowledge and, 102 (*see also* sexuality education); social influence and, 12–14, 101; story content and, 66–67, 68. *See also* age-variant sexual activity; fantasies; self-stimulation; sex-play
Child Study Association, 31
Christianity, 120
Christian Right, 128
circumcision, 120–21
Conn, J. H., 10, 66
Constantine, L. L., 128–29
Croft, C. A., 109
cult of innocence, 102

Davis, Katherine B., 26
Deisher, R. W., 53
DeMause, L., 120
Denmark, 117
Dolgin, B. L., 123–24
Dolgin, J. L., 123–24

English Anti-Slavery Society, 95
Ennew, J., 95, 96
erotic orientation, 11
Examples of Hostile Environmental Sexual Harassment, 137

fantasies: aggression and, 67–68, 69–70; content of, 67–71; genital play and, 66; masturbation and, 69–71; sexual knowledge and, 65, 102; social inhibitions and, 66
Finkelhor, D., 87, 90, 94
Ford, C. S., 57
Fraiberg, S., 10–11
Freud, Sigmund, 10, 11, 14, 36, 89, 102

Gagnon, J., 23, 31–32, 75
Galenson, E., 21, 23
Gardner, R.–A., 67, 68
gender comparison: on adolescent sexual activity, 41; on masturbation, 28–29, 30–31, 71; on oral

sex-play, 54; on preadolescent sex-play, 40, 43–44; on same-sex sex-play, 57–58, 59, 61, 62; on sexual activity, 53; on sexual talk, 42–43, 45–46; on story content, 66–67, 68
Gilbert, N., 88
Giovacchini, P. L., 89
Goldman, J., 72–73, 87, 117, 133–34
Goldman, R., 72–73, 87, 117, 133–34
Greece, 120
Guidelines for Sexuality Education: Kindergarten—12th Grade, 110–13
Gundersen, B. H., 37, 45
Guyon, Rene, 15, 91

Halverson, H. M., 9
homosexuality, 62–63, 120
hypnotic role taking, 7

incest, 90–91, 93, 124–25, 126
India, 53, 83
infant-mother relationship: attachment process and, 4, 5–6; breast-feeding and, 8; child development literature and, 10–11; child's dependence and, 2; communication and, 4–5, 6–7; eye contact and, 6; facial expressions and, 5; genital play and, 22; hypnotic role taking and, 7–8; initial contact and, 3; interaction time and, 7; newborn's resources and, 3–4; physical intimacy and, 4, 7, 11; reciprocal development and, 7; vocalization and, 6

Johnson, T. C., 15
Johnson, V. E., 10, 14
Johnston, C., 53
Kalvin, H., Jr., 124
Kanner, L., 10
Kaplan, H. S., 14, 103
Kempe, C. H., 88
Kennell, D. H., 3
Kilpatrick, A. C., 86 87

Kinsey, A. C., et al., study by: female sex-play and, 40; first ejaculation and, 55n; infant orgasms and, 23; masturbation and, 25, 27–31; masturbation fantasies and, 71; preadolescent intercourse and, 53; same-sex sex-play and, 58, 59, 61, 62; sexual permissiveness and, 84–85; two-year-olds' intimacy and, 36
Klaus, H. M., 3
Kline, D., 23
Knuckman, Paul, 96
Kryso, J., 90

LaHaye, B., 128
LaHaye, T., 128
Langfeldt, Thore, 27–28, 30–31
laws. *See* child (sex) laws
Lee, J. A., 119–20
Levin, S., 69
Levine, H., 30, 101, 134
Levine, M. I., 21, 23–24, 28, 31, 32
Lewis, W. C., 7
Luria, Z., 42, 46

Maccoby, E. E., 30, 101, 134
Man/Boy Lovers of America, 125
Maryland, 124
Masters, W. H., 10, 14
masturbation: age differences and, 30; control of, 120; discovery of, 28–29; effects of, 28, 31; fantasies and, 69–71; by females, 26–27; frequency of, 31; gender comparison on, 28–29, 30–31; genital play and, 21, 23–24; guilt feeling and, 26–27, 31; parental attitudes on, 31–32; prevalence of, 23, 30; same-sex sex-play and, 60; satisfaction from, 25–26, 27; Scandinavia and, 27; by three-year-olds, 24–25, 28; via thigh pressure, 29–30
maternal sensitivity, 3
Melanesia, 83
Minnesota, 136–37
Mittelman, M., 95

Model Penal Code, 122
Money, J., 126

National Center on Child Abuse and Neglect, 95, 125–26
National Council for Mental Health, 128–29
Netherlands, 94–95, 121, 128–29
New Guinea, 57
New York, 125
New Zealand, 83
Norway, 30–31, 37–38, 45

Panama, 84
Papago, 84
Parents Liberation, 16
Pedophile Information Exchange, 125
pedophilia, 93–95, 125
Philo, 120
Pitcher, E. G., 67, 68
Pollock, L. A., 130
pornography, 46, 70
pornography, child, 95–96, 126
preadolescents, 80–81
preadolescent sex-play: adult supervision and, 46; cross-gender chasing and, 45; crushes and, 43; dancing and, 50–51; dating and, 47–49; exhibition and, 41–42; by females, 40; gender comparison on, 40, 43–44; gender consciousness and, 39–40; genital fondling and, 51–52; intercourse and, 53; kissing and, 49–50; making-out and, 51; male stimulation and, 40; mixed parties and, 46–47; oral sex and, 54; pornography and, 46; pregnancies and, 55; puberty and, 41; sexual talk and, 45–46; socio-educational status and, 53; teasing and, 44–45
Prelinger, E., 67, 68
Project on Human Sexual Development, 62
prostitution, 96–97

Rainwater, Lee, 80–81, 102
Ramsey, G. V., 30, 31, 40, 51, 53, 67
Reich, Wilhelm, 91

Rene Guyon Society, 16
Renshaw, D. C., 91
Roberts, E. J., 23
Roiphe, H., 21, 23
Rome, 120

St. Louis, Missouri, 80–81
same-sex sex-play: age differences and, 58; cultural differences and, 57; exhibition and, 58–59; frequency of, 58; gender comparison on, 57–58, 59, 61, 62; genital manipulation and, 59–61; homosexual tendency and, 62–63; number of participants and, 58; object insertion and, 61; oral sex and, 61; parental attitudes on, 62–63; social accessibility and, 62
Sandfort, T.G.M., 94–95
Sattel, Sue, 137
Scandinavia, 27, 38, 123, 136. *See also names of Scandinavian countries*
Scanzoni, J., 129
Schaefer, Leah C., 22–23, 25, 26, 27
Sears, R. R., 30, 101, 134
self-stimulation: age of initial, 21; climax attainment and, 26; via genital play, 21–22, 23–24; via rhythmic manipulation, 22–23, 27–28. *See also* masturbation
sex play: bodily exploration and, 37–38; boys' genitals and, 37; cultural influence and, 38, 52–53; curiosity and, 36–37; defined, 35; girls' genitals and, 38; parental attitudes on, 39; prevalence of, 37, 38; remembrance of, 38–39; simulated intercourse and, 52. *See also* preadolescent sex-play; same-sex sex-play
Sexual Freedom League, 16
sexual harassment, 136, 137
sexual knowledge: age-variant sexual activity and, 80–82, 85–86; fantasies and, 65; fantasy content and, 102; Sweden and, 72, 73. *See also* sexuality education

sexual misuse, 95
sexual violence, 136–37
sexuality education: age and, 109, 113, 135; age-variant sexual activity and, 86; child sexual abuse and, 136; condom use and, 114; conservative influence and, 115–16, 136; content of, 109–14; developmental perspective and, 104; family values and, 107–8, 117; focus on sexuality and, 116, 117; future direction of, 137; lack of, 101–4; negative emphasis and, 113–14, 115, 116, 135, 136; parental confusion and, 108; parental denial of, 104–5, 134; from parents, 105–7, 117; from peers, 108, 135; positive results from, 105–7, 135; protective paradigm and, 130; from school, 108–13, 134, 135–36; from social elders, 80–81; Sweden-U.S. comparison on, 134–35; task force guidelines for, 110–13; teacher qualification and, 114–15, 116; teenage pregnancies and, 116–17
sexually transmitted diseases (STDs), 116, 135
sodomy, 57
South Africa, 83
South America, 84
Spiro, M. E., 36
Spitz, R. A., 14, 22
statutory rape, 121–22, 124
The Study Group of New York, 12
Summit, R., 90
Sweden: abortion rates in, 135; sex-play attitudes in, 38; sexual knowledge and, 72, 73; sexuality education in, 114, 117, 121, 134, 135; teenage pregnancies and, 117
Swift, Carolyn, 127

Tanganyika, 84
teenage pregnancies, 116–17, 135
Thorne, B., 42, 44, 46
Tisza, V. B., 95, 126–27
Trobriand Island, 53
Tsukada, G. K., 92

Udry, J. R., 136
Ullertsam, L., 125
United States: abuse definition and, 87–88; child liberation movement in, 16; child sex talk and, 66; high school sex and, 114; premarital intercourse in, 135; protective child-raising in, 12–13, 16, 84, 101–2; sex law diversity in, 122; sex-play and, 38, 57, 58, 83; sexuality education in, 108, 113, 134–35; statutory rape and, 122; teenage pregnancies in, 116

Victims of Child Abuse Laws (VOCAL), 126

Wermer, H., 69
When Children Ask About Sex, 31
Wolf, K. W., 22

Yates, A., 14–15, 24

Zeisel, H., 124

About the Author

FLOYD M. MARTINSON is Research Professor of Sociology at Gustavus Adolphus College in Minnesota. He is the author of five books including *Family and Society* (1970), *Children and Sex* (1981), and *Growing up in Norway* (1992), and was recently appointed to the Editorial Advisory Board of *The Journal of Sex Research*.

HQ 784 .S45 M37 1994
MARTINSON, FLOYD MANSFILD,
1916-
THE SEXUAL LIFE OF CHILDREN

DATE DUE

AUG 21 '95			
DEC 8 '97			

Demco, Inc. 38-293